Those Who Are Offended

Dag Heward-Mills

Parchment House

Unless otherwise stated, all Scripture quotations are taken from the
King James Version of the Bible

THOSE WHO ARE OFFENDED

Copyright © 2022 Dag Heward-Mills

Published by Parchment House 2022
1st Printing 2022

Find out more about Dag Heward-Mills
Healing Jesus Campaign
Write to: evangelist@daghewardmills.org
Website: www.daghewardmills.org
Facebook: Dag Heward-Mills
Twitter: @EvangelistDag

ISBN: 978-1-64330-511-0

All rights reserved under international copyright law.
Written permission must be secured from the publisher to
use or reproduce any part of this book.

Contents

1. There Will Be Offences 1
2. Offended: Those Who Are Rebuked and Corrected 7
3. Offended: Those Who Turn into Monsters 19
4. Offended: Those Who Are Rejected 28
5. Offended: Those Who Are Sacked 31
6. Offended: Those Who Are Offended by Greatness 35
7. Offended: Those Who Cannot Handle Hard Sayings 42
8. Offended: Those Who Cannot Handle Trouble in the Leader's Life 46
9. Offended: Those Who Are Abused 51
10. Offence: Weapon of Satan 54
11. Stage of Offence: Withdrawal 58
12. Stage of Offence: Resentment 65
13. Stage of Offence: Mistrust and Suspicion 68
14. Stage of Offence: Malice, Ill-Will 72
15. Stage of Offence: Stubbornness 77
16. Stage of Offence: Treachery 80
17. Stage of Offence: Demonization 83
18. Offences: How to Overcome Them 87
19. How to Protect Yourself from Being Offended 97

CHAPTER 1

There Will Be Offences

Woe unto the world because of offences! For it must needs be that offences come; but woe to that man by whom the offence cometh!

Matthew 18:7

1. There will be offences that will hurt you.

You may be happy to be a member of the church today. You may be glad that God has called you and made you a part of the fold. You may be an excited member of a Church Council. You and your friends may be glad that you are a part of the family.

Indeed, you may even boast about how things are different in your church. You may speak confidently about how others do not have the blessings that you have.

But Jesus has predicted that one day you will be struck in such a way that you have a lot of pain. This pain may be emotional pain. This pain may be pain in your heart. This hurt may be something you find difficult to get rid of.

Jesus has predicted that you will soon have experiences that will cause you much pain. The pain you will experience may change your life forever.

2. There will be offences that will anger you.

You may be happy today. You may enjoy the church today! You may be excited about what God is doing in the ministry. Jesus is predicting, according to the scripture, that something may happen that is going to irritate, annoy and anger you.

Jesus has predicted that you will one day have a set of experiences that will irritate, annoy or anger you.

What can annoy you? What could irritate you? What is there that could anger you in the future?

You must expect this event of pain to unfold soon. Heaven and earth will pass away but His words will not pass away.

3. There will be offences that will produce resentment and hatred.

There are events in life that will cause you great displeasure. Indeed, these events may be so tumultuous that they may even generate hatred in you. Hate is a very strong emotion. Hatred comes before murder. When people are offended, you get the feeling that they would even like to kill you.

What sort of experiences could generate hatred and resentment in a happy person like you? You are so full of passion, love and zeal today. What could hurt you so badly that you will develop such a strong dislike for someone? I have had people who have described me as the nicest, greatest and best. These same people have turned around, after being offended, and called me the exact opposite.

I have had people who were so happy with me and ascribed all the good things in their lives to the fact that they knew me and were ministered to by me. When these same people were hurt, I heard them say they wished they had never met me in this world. I have also had people who have called me the most anointed person they knew and then after they were hurt, called me satan. Obviously, these people experienced something so terrible that it completely changed their perspective of me.

One day, I had a series of experiences that built up in me until I developed resentment and hatred for the offenders. I noticed the new feeling of resentment and hatred welling up in me. This was indeed a new experience. Up till then, I had never found it difficult to forgive or overcome bad experiences.

Indeed, that bad experience was changing me and changing my attitude completely. It was something I noticed because it was a completely new feeling I had not experienced before. I immediately had to check myself and stop myself from continuing to feel that way.

4. There will be offences that will be difficult to forgive and forget.

It is important to know that there are things that everyone finds difficult to forgive. What will offend you and prevent you from forgiving may be very different from what offends me. Something that causes a big offence is not necessarily a big event. For instance, I may transfer you from London to the backend of Democratic Republic of Congo. But that may not offend you. On the other hand, there may be a meeting in the office from which you are excluded. The exclusion from the meeting may strike you on the wrong chord. A great offence may start developing in you because you feel rejected, unwanted and unaccepted.

It is important to understand that there are things that will offend you. You may think to yourself, "This does not offend me! That does not offend me!" You may be married and declare, "I am not offended or worried if my husband has affairs with other women."

Even if you are so resilient, I assure you that there is something that you will find difficult to forgive. It is not possible to come into this world and never be offended. It is not possible to come into this world and never have an experience that you find difficult to forgive.

The root of bitterness is available for every unforgiving person. You must expect to have these experiences because Jesus said you would have them.

5. There will be offences that will bring problems.

All the problems in this world come from offended people. People are angered and bitter from experiences that they have had in life. People have bad experiences in churches, in ministries and in fellowships.

These bad experiences that bring hurts, pain and bitterness are the foundations of tragic breakaways and rebellion in the church. Rarely do you find a breakaway person or a rebel or a discontented person who has not been offended. All grumblers and murmurers are full of offence.

"Woe to the world" means "Trouble to the world." All difficulties, all challenges and all wars in the world can be traced to some kind of offence.

The First World War was started because the Archduke Franz Ferdinand of Austria was killed by some radical independents.

The Second World War was started because Adolf Hitler felt that the Germans had been given a bad deal at the end of the First World War in the Treaty of Versailles. His reference to this war and how it ended unfairly for the Germans was the reason for his starting a Second World War.

As you can see, the world is really in danger because people are hurt and offended. No one is exempted from the scourge of offence. Apostle Paul was offended many times in his ministry.

Who is weak, and I am not weak? who is offended, and I burn not?

2 Corinthians 11:29

You cannot continue for long in the ministry without having a good reason to be offended. People speak with such great conviction about their hurts and offences. Jesus predicted offences! I can remember many occasions when I could have left the church. I have been offended many times. Indeed, I could say with Paul, "Who is offended and I burn not?" Each offence you experience is an opportunity to turn you into a monster.

You must keep your spirit pure and free of offence lest you metamorphose into the exact opposite of what you have believed.

6. There will be offences that will bring woes.

Woe to the church because of offences! Almost every difficult character that has caused trouble in the church has been offended by something. You just have to go into the history of a matter and you will find out when, where and how a person became offended.

Churches that experience splits will tell you that somebody somewhere was very offended and veered off on his own, railing accusations at the leadership of the church.

I am grateful to God for your happy church. I am excited that God has raised you up to do such wonders. But I can predict that it is only a matter of time before offence will arise in the congregation. Some of the pastors who are loyal today will become disloyal because they will be offended. Jesus said offences would definitely come. It is your duty to stabilize yourself and be fully persuaded about what you believe.

Offence is a turning point in your life. Offence is an emergency! Like a snake that causes people to quickly rise up to kill it, offence must be dealt with as swiftly as it rears its head.

Great peace have they which love thy law: and nothing shall offend them.

Psalm 119:165

CHAPTER 2

Offended: Those Who Are Rebuked and Corrected

He that reproveth a scorner getteth to himself shame: and he that rebuketh a wicked man getteth himself a blot. REPROVE NOT A SCORNER, LEST HE HATE THEE: rebuke a wise man, and he will love thee. Give instruction to a wise man, and he will be yet wiser: teach a just man, and he will increase in learning.

Proverbs 9:7-9

The scripture is clear that rebuking someone is a risky business. People love to be praised and pampered. Most people do not take well to correction. When people are being corrected, most of them fail to think of what they have done wrong.

Whenever you have to correct someone, you must be careful that the person does not get offended. Indeed, you must avoid correcting people who are not mature enough to receive correction.

It is amazing to see how people react to rebukes and correction. I remember a brother who had defiled a young lady. When he was rebuked and corrected, he went off huffing and puffing, saying that he had received a wound in his soul. He went on to say that he would never recover from that wound and that he would die with that wound.

Instead of this brother repenting from abusing and violating people's wives, he turned around and accused those who were trying to offer him correction.

Indeed, correction is grievous and painful to men of error. "Correction is grievous unto him that forsaketh the way: and he that hateth reproof shall die" (Proverbs 15:10).

Decide that you will never be one of those who cannot receive correction humbly. Receiving correction is one of the important spiritual tablets that you must swallow if you will ever amount to anything in the ministry. Decide to think about your role in the issue at stake. Do not think about whether somebody is raising his voice or waving his left hand at you. Do not think about whether others received the same level of correction when they did something wrong.

Decide to be someone who simply receives correction. Decide that you will not answer back or have a counter claim or a counter suit against the person who is correcting you. Decide to be humble! Decide to be mature! Only then will you do well!

Therefore thou shalt speak all these words unto them; but they will not hearken to thee: thou shalt also call unto them; but they will not answer thee. But thou shalt say unto them, this is a nation that obeyeth not the voice of the Lord their God, NOR RECEIVETH CORRECTION: truth is perished, and is cut off from their mouth.

Jeremiah 7:27-28

Correction is against human nature. Because the nature of man is to proclaim his goodness (Proverbs 20:6), there are many varying responses to rebukes from Christians. There are very good responses and indeed there are very bad responses. Good responses range from mature acceptance of correction to the other extreme of hatred and revenge on the one who corrected you. A good response to being rebuked comes from what you think about the person who is correcting you.

1. **People hate rebuke and correction because rebukes shame and reduce them in the eyes of men.**

   When thou with rebukes dost correct man for iniquity, thou makest his beauty to consume away like a moth: surely every man is vanity. Selah.

   Psalm 39:11

   People hate to be rebuked because rebukes make their beauty vanish. A person who is rebuked or corrected is lowered in the eyes of men and looks far less glamorous than he would like to be. Imagine a man standing to be corrected by the boss in front of everyone. This man may not take this lightly. He may begin to resent the correction that is being meted out.

2. **People only want to be praised so they naturally do not want to be rebuked.**

   Most men will proclaim every one his own goodness: but a faithful man who can find?

   Proverbs 20:6

People see themselves as good. I think that is why we only say good things about ourselves. Whenever a person narrates a story, you must be aware that he is going to say good things about himself. He will never really say the negative role he played in whatever happened.

You can expect to hear the good aspects and have the evil, cruel, nasty and unpleasant parts nicely avoided in the narrative. At best most people are silent on their sins and faults.

Notice the wisdom of Solomon! Solomon knew that men proclaim their goodness (Proverbs 20:6).

3. **Allow rebukes and correction to purge out evil from you.**

The blueness of a wound cleanseth away evil: so do stripes the inward parts of the belly.

Proverbs 20:30

Evil will not be purged out from you until you see and understand why you are being corrected or rebuked. Indeed the "blueness" of the wound, which is the sign of the punishment in your life indicates how much you have been corrected and received understanding.

Evil is purged when you gain understanding! The timing of understanding is usually linked to the timing of removal of evil.

4. **You must respect and reverence correction.**

Furthermore we have had fathers of our flesh which corrected us, and we gave them reverence: shall we not much rather be in subjection unto the Father of spirits, and live?

Hebrews 12:9

When God corrects people they often take it lightly only to repeat the very same act again many years later. A rebuke in your youth is the great warning from God about something that would like to destroy you one day. Many trivialize rebukes and corrections to their own destruction. Many feel that it is not a necessary experience. Many call for the end of their punishment long before it should be ended.

Calling for a shortening of your punishment reveals you have little understanding of the depths of evil you were into – "Oh, I understand what you are saying. There is no need to keep on talking!" "Oh I understand what you are saying, there is no need for me to be transferred from here or to receive any other punitive measures."

5. Rebukes and correction are the stamp of ownership and the stamp of the love of a father.

If ye endure chastening, God dealeth with you as with sons; for what son is he whom the father chasteneth not? But if ye be without chastisement, whereof all are partakers, then are ye bastards, and not sons.

Hebrews 12:7-8

You could decide to view correction and rebuke as a special line of relationship which you have with God. Correction will open up a new dimension of your relationship with the authority figure in your life.

You will learn how love is mature and not just full of praises and deception. One man of God said the people who did him most good in his life were the people who told him what was wrong with him.

A good response to being rebuked is to think or believe that someone is loving you. Unfortunately, when people are corrected, they think they are being hated, rejected and disliked.

6. Not receiving correction makes you one of the worst kinds of Christians ever.

Woe to her that is filthy and polluted, to the oppressing city! She obeyed not the voice; SHE RECEIVED NOT

CORRECTION; she trusted not in the Lord; she drew not near to her God.

Zephaniah 3:1-2

People who don't receive correction well can become like devils. The Bible is full of warnings about how important it is to receive correction and rebukes.

7. Not receiving correction properly reveals a lack of endurance.

If ye endure chastening, God dealeth with you as with sons; for what son is he whom the father chasteneth not?

Hebrews 12:7

A lack of endurance is a lack of Christian character. Endurance is mentioned in many places as a key Christian quality that must be developed. Above all, endurance is a key quality of love. To go through things, to survive things, to persevere through trying times is a major element of the Christian life. Always remember that love endures all things. If you cannot endure correction, you cannot endure anything in the ministry. Many make shipwreck of their faith because they cannot endure correction, rebukes, or something unpleasant being told to them.

Beareth all things, believeth all things, hopeth all things, endureth all things.

1 Corinthians 13:7

Do you want to end your future ministry because you were shouted at? Do you want to end your whole ministry because something unpleasant was said to you at a meeting? Then what are you made of?

Do you know how many unpleasant things will be said about you just because you've decided to serve God? You are a man of straw if you cannot endure corrections, transfers or rebukes.

Learn these four rules of endurance in ministry that Paul reveals to Timothy:

a. Endure the hardness of rebukes and correction that is necessary for your life and ministry. Being corrected is hard! That is why you are asked to endure hardness! Correction, rebukes and reproof are the way of life. That is also the harder way. Endure the hardness of rebukes without destroying yourself.

> Thou therefore endure hardness, as a good soldier of Jesus Christ.
>
> 2 Timothy 2:3

b. Endure all things that God allows you to go through, whatever they may be. Endure all and not some of the things. Enduring some things will not let the correction seep in and change your life.

> Therefore I endure all things for the elect's sakes, that they may also obtain the salvation which is in Christ Jesus with eternal glory.
>
> 2 Timothy 2:10

c. Endure the afflictions of punishment. There will be persecutions against you. There will be afflictions because you are God's servant.

> Persecutions, afflictions, which came unto me at Antioch, at Iconium, at Lystra; what persecutions I endured: but out of them all the Lord delivered me.
>
> 2 Timothy 3:11

d. Endure sound and good teachings. Why would you have to endure sound teaching? Because really good teaching does not just praise you. People want to have praises heaped upon their heads. People want to hear that good things are going to happen to them. People want to hear nice things only. But indeed sound preaching and good teaching always involve a lot of reproving rebuking and correcting.

For the time will come when they will not endure sound doctrine; but after their own lusts shall they heap to themselves teachers, having itching ears;

2 Timothy 4:3

Notice how Paul teaches that the scripture should be used. It must be used to correct, to reprove. to rebuke and to nail home the truths from God's word that are difficult to bear or even hear.

All scripture is given by inspiration of God, and is profitable for doctrine, for reproof, for correction for instruction in righteousness:

2 Timothy 3:16

I once knew a sister who had two pastors. She would listen to them both but eventually fell in love with the counsel and teachings that came from the smooth sounding pastor. She forsook the teacher who was giving her sound doctrine, correcting her and rebuking her constantly. She became totally immersed in the smooth talking, teaching and counselling that was heaped on her. Indeed with time she grew to resent the teacher who told her hard things and totally gave herself to the teacher who seemed to be telling her nice things. Her smooth talking pastor even told her that she was being maltreated by the other teacher because of his stance in various scripture.

Deception is real! Truth is hard! Truth is sometimes nasty. Truth about us is often difficult to believe or bear. Eventually, the smooth-talking teacher destroyed this immature sister. When she found out that he had smooth-talked her into destruction, she could not believe what had happened to her. But she would not have been deceived if she was just willing to receive correction and rebukes which were due her as part of growing up in the Lord.

I can understand why a person would surround themselves such people. It is indeed far nicer to hear smooth and sweet talk that justifies you and makes you feel good even though you are wrong about everything. Be forewarned and do not become an example of someone having itching ears who heaps to himself teachers who tell him what he want to hear.

Your ministry will never come forth into its fullest bloom until you endure certain hard rebukes, reproofs and correction.

8. Correction and rebukes can lead to dishonour.

He who corrects a scoffer gets dishonor for himself, And he who reproves a wicked man gets insults for himself.
Proverbs 9:7 (NASB 1995)

I have been dishonoured mostly by people I rebuked and corrected. In the course of raising up thousands of pastors and being a spiritual father to many, you would expect there would be some corrections and some rebukes.

Most of the people I have corrected have taken it well. But indeed some of them rose up strongly to insult me and to dishonour me. I was called "Satan" by someone whom I corrected and would not allow him to have his way. This is nothing new! When pride fills a person, he is easily offended. Easy offence takes place when a person is puffed up in pride. A swollen toad is more easily pricked or stepped on than a small one. A puffed up balloon easier to burst and be destroyed.

When people are proud and swollen the slightest prick causes an explosion. A balloon that is being inflated is not really that size. It is actually a small piece of rubber. But its inflated state makes it look much bigger than it actually is.

Inflated pastors have an illusion and a delusion of how big they really are. Sometimes they have had opportunities that have swelled up their minds. They think much more highly of themselves than they really are.

Many successful people are actually the products of many other people's input. Pride blinds you to the things that others have done to make you what you are.

Many successful people are actually the products of a set of circumstances that have come together in perfect timing to make you look successful. This is what someone would call grace or luck.

Whichever it is, it is a reality that your greatness is merely an act of grace, mercy and love from God. Rising up, in great confidence about who you are and what you can do, is a sign that you are deceived about who you really are. Such proud people are easy to offend. The offence itself is the sign of the presence of pride. "Who do you think you are to say something like that to me? Why should you call me to a meeting to answer questions?"

One fellow said he would not want to be the subject of any meetings or discussions so he would prefer to resign than to sit through any more enquiries into his ministry work. Indeed, such declarations reveal the "bigness" of the person in his own eyes.

Pride leads to much offence. When a man can rebuke, insult and degrade his own father, he is indeed proud and too big to remain under his father. A father's rebuke can cause a proud person to insult him and to break God's eternal and sacred commandments of honouring fathers.

9. Rebukes can lead to hatred and bitterness.

Do not rebuke mockers or THEY WILL HATE YOU; rebuke the wise and they will love you.

Proverbs 9:8 (NIV)

Hatred is the final and the worst development in the life of someone who takes correction badly. As you can see clearly, the word of God tells us that people hate you for correcting them.

Hatred is the culmination of unforgiveness and bitterness for being rebuked. Hatred reveals malice and a desire to harm someone. I have experienced intense hatred from pastors and leaders who once worked with me. Most of these fellows were corrected about something or the other. There are times I would wonder, "What have I done to these people? Why do they hate me so much?"

One time I was at a crusade and preaching every night. Even as I was preaching I could feel the hatred of an individual I had corrected and rebuked. In the middle of a sermon I stopped and asked a bystander why I was hated so much. Indeed the pride, hatred and wickedness in the person was manifest without reason.

Hatred in its purest form often doesn't have a reason for its existence. Jesus experienced pure, livid hatred.

But this cometh to pass, that the word might be fulfilled that is written in their law, they hated me without a cause.

John 15:25

When there are reasons for the hatred, you don't have pure hatred. But when there is mindless malice and wickedness with hatred, you can tell that you have met pure hatred. A hater wants you to die. A hater is malicious, damaging and spiteful. A hater wants to kill you and do something really harmful to you. A hater wants to exact revenge on you. That is all you will feel the day you meet real hatred. Be careful because there are people who will kill you if you give them a chance.

Whosoever hateth his brother is a murderer: and ye know that no murderer hath eternal life abiding in him.

1 John 3:15

For your own sake, you must never allow unforgiveness and bitterness to grow in you because it may develop into hatred. I have met many people with hatred. Both men and women can be filled with hatred and try to destroy you. Perhaps the worst kind of hatred is that from those to whom you have ministered and done many good things.

Jesus asked a question which revealed that hatred, is a high-level, spiritual, everlasting thing that has no logical basis. Jesus asked why people hated Him so much and wanted to kill Him.

Jesus answered them, Many good works have I shewed you from my Father; for which of those works do ye stone me?

John 10:32

Hatred does not make sense! It is an intense dislike for a person and an equally intense desire to destroy someone. Hatred is a desire for cruelty to be inflicted on someone. Hatred is satan personified! Perhaps hatred is borne out of a desire to revenge on a person for daring to correct or rebuke you.

CHAPTER 3

Offended: Those Who Turn into Monsters

And it shall come to pass in the last days, that the mountain of the Lord's house shall be established in the top of the mountains, and shall be exalted above the hills; and all nations shall flow unto it. And many people shall go and say, Come ye, and let us go up to the mountain of the Lord, to the house of the God of Jacob; and he will teach us of his ways, and we will walk in his paths: for out of Zion shall go forth the law, and the word of the Lord from Jerusalem. AND HE SHALL JUDGE AMONG THE NATIONS, AND SHALL REBUKE MANY PEOPLE: and they shall beat their swords into plowshares, and their spears into pruninghooks: nation shall not lift up sword against nation, neither shall they learn war any more.

Isaiah 2:2-4

Instead of turning into a monster when you are rebuked, you must ask yourself whether the rebukes have a basis or not. What is your role in the problem that has arisen? Instead of being offended, you must accept the rebukes in good faith. Rebukes and corrections are found all through the Bible. You can never escape from genuine rebukes and correction, once you are in the church.

The scripture above shows us that God will build His church in the last days. The house of the Lord will be established on the top of the mountains and exalted above the hills. The church will be an international place. The church will be outstanding and many people will come to it. The law of God and the word of the Lord will come forth from the mountain of the Lord's house. Also, God will rebuke many people.

If you want to be part of the mountain of the Lord's house, you must be ready to receive many rebukes. You are not a part of God's house to receive praises and pampering. When you come to the house of the Lord, expect to receive the law of God, the judgment of God and also the rebukes.

Do not allow the rebukes and the corrections of God's word to turn you into a monster. Allow God's word to have its perfect work. Remember that scripture does not exist to pamper you. Nor does scripture exist to praise you. It exists to inspire you, to teach you doctrine, to reprove you, to correct you and to instruct you. You cannot come to God without being rebuked.

All scripture is given by inspiration of God, and is profitable for doctrine, for reproof, for correction, for instruction in righteousness:

2 Timothy 3:16

Accept that painful corrections and sharp rebukes will be part of your life if you are at a place where the scripture is taught and preached in truth. I am sad to report to you that many people do not take rebukes well. This means that many people do not take a large part of the word of God well.

==If you do not flow with the rebukes, you do not flow with God. If you do not flow with corrective measures, you do not flow with most of God's words.==

In this chapter, we will see that people who are rebuked are often offended and turn into monsters.

A "monster" is someone who has deviated grotesquely from the natural, normal form. It is amazing that when the truth is confronted and addressed by an authority figure, people get terribly offended and metamorphose into monsters. People who are offended turn into frightful, shocking and outrageous versions of themselves.

Pastors who are offended turn into shocking variations of what they used to be before they were offended.

Christians who are offended turn into something so different that they are unrecognizable.

Do not allow yourself to turn into a monster when you are corrected and rebuked. You will deviate grotesquely from the normal, if you do not respond properly to rebukes and corrections. I want you to see three monsters that were created out of rebukes and corrections. The three examples in this chapter are the most frightening examples of people who changed into grotesque evil creatures because they were rebuked, corrected and reproved in truth and in the Spirit!

1. Herod the Monster

> BUT WHEN JOHN REBUKED HEROD THE TETRARCH BECAUSE OF HIS MARRIAGE to Herodias, his brother's wife, and all the other evil things he had done, Herod added this to them all: He locked John up in prison.
>
> Luke 3:19-20 (NIV)

Herod was rebuked by John because of his marriage to Herodias, and he became someone who fought against God's prophet. Herod was someone who could go as far as attacking

God's prophet and imprisoning him. Herod became a prophet killer because he was rebuked about his marriage.

Jesus said John the Baptist was the greatest person born of a woman. That is a serious statement to make about any human being. Yet, he was brutally murdered by a monster called Herod. Herod became the killer of the greatest person born of a woman.

> Verily I say unto you, Among them that are born of women there hath not risen a greater than John the Baptist: notwithstanding he that is least in the kingdom of heaven is greater than he.
>
> Matthew 11:11

This is what rebukes and corrections can do to someone who does not take it well. Offended people turn into monsters and commit ultimate evils. I have seen pastors who were dear sons, turn around and commit ultimate evils.

Some who called me "father" turned around and called me "satan". I have had people who honoured me for years as a father turn around and say that I was the worst thing that ever happened to them and they wish they had never met me.

2. Herod's Wife the Monster

> For Herod had laid hold on John, and bound him, and put him in prison for Herodias' sake, his brother Philip's wife. FOR JOHN SAID UNTO HIM, IT IS NOT LAWFUL FOR THEE TO HAVE HER. And when he would have put him to death, he feared the multitude, because they counted him as a prophet. But when Herod's birthday was kept, the daughter of Herodias danced before them, and pleased Herod. Whereupon he promised with an oath to give her whatsoever she would ask. AND SHE, BEING BEFORE INSTRUCTED OF HER MOTHER, SAID, GIVE ME HERE JOHN BAPTIST'S HEAD IN A CHARGER.
>
> Matthew 14:3-8

Herod's wife is another example of someone who turned into a monster. Herod's wife was a regular woman who was having an affair; but because the relationship was rebuked by John the Baptist, she turned into a man killer. A regular woman turned into a murderess. This is a picture of a "sexy girlfriend" to Herod who had turned into a monster and wanted a plate covered with blood and bearing the chopped-off head of a human being.

3. The Pharisees and Scribes, the Monsters

> **Woe unto you, scribes and Pharisees, hypocrites! for ye pay tithe of mint and anise and cummin, and have omitted the weightier matters of the law, judgment, mercy, and faith: these ought ye to have done, and not to leave the other undone. Ye blind guides, which strain at a gnat, and swallow a camel.**
>
> **Woe unto you, scribes and Pharisees, hypocrites! for ye make clean the outside of the cup and of the platter, but within they are full of extortion and excess.**
>
> **Matthew 23:23-25**

Jesus asked the thousands of disciples who were listening to Him whether they were offended. He knew that offence would turn them into monsters. Indeed, the scribes and Pharisees did become monsters. A "monster" is someone who has deviated grotesquely from the normal and expected form. The Pharisees and scribes were expected to be men of kindness, men of love, men with a good heart. Instead, they became men of envy, men of hatred, full of treachery and murder. Today, the term "scribes and Pharisees" denotes an evil religious group.

The scribes and Pharisees were men of piety, men of holiness and men of religion. They turned into monsters that murdered Jesus Christ the holy Son of God because they were offended by His rebukes and the reproofs.

In Matthew 23, Jesus rebuked the Pharisees about many things. He called them vipers, serpents and dead men's tombs.

He called them hypocrites, He called them fools and He called them blind guides. Jesus called the Pharisees and scribes the children of hell.

These rebukes and reproofs greatly offended the Pharisees and scribes. The offended Pharisees and scribes became the murderers of the Son of God. They became the monsters who crucified the Son of God.

Be careful of offence! Be careful of rebukes and reproofs when they come! Be careful of correction!

I want you to notice some of the rebukes of Jesus Christ. He simply said, "If I do not do the works of my Father do not believe me." Believe in the works that you see Me doing even if you don't believe in Me as a person. This simple, but truthful logic provoked hatred and anger in the hearers. Jesus' life was in danger from the murderous, angry and offended Pharisees.

> If I do not the works of my Father, believe me not. But if I do, though ye believe not me, believe the works: that ye may know, and believe, that the Father is in me, and I in him. THEREFORE THEY SOUGHT AGAIN TO TAKE HIM: BUT HE ESCAPED OUT OF THEIR HAND,
>
> John 10:37-39

On another occasion, Jesus spoke about how He was not honouring Himself. He spoke about how He existed before Abraham came into the world. The truth was too much for certain people. They hated Him for the truths that He told them. They took up stones to kill Him but Jesus hid Himself. (Stoning was the favourite method for killing in those days.) Never forget that rebuking and reproving people generates such hatred that people are turned into monsters.

> Jesus answered, If I honour myself, my honour is nothing: it is my Father that honoureth me; of whom ye say, that he is your God: Yet ye have not known him; but I know him: and if I should say, I know him not, I shall be a liar like unto you: but I know him, and keep his saying. Your

father Abraham rejoiced to see my day: and he saw it, and was glad. Then said the Jews unto him, Thou art not yet fifty years old, and hast thou seen Abraham? Jesus said unto them, Verily, verily, I say unto you, Before Abraham was, I am. THEN TOOK THEY UP STONES TO CAST AT HIM: BUT JESUS HID HIMSELF, and went out of the temple, going through the midst of them, and so passed by.

John 8:54-59

Jesus spoke about the works that He did in His Father's name. Jesus had performed astounding healings and miracles in His Father's name. He rebuked the Pharisees and scribes by pointing them to the supernatural power and miracles that were following His ministry. Explain that if you can! The logic of His clear answers and explanations was the sharpest rebuke ever. The people standing around were convinced about the emptiness of the ministry of the Pharisees and scribes. "And many of the people believed on him, and said, When Christ cometh, will he do more miracles than these which this man hath done? The Pharisees heard that the people murmured such things concerning him; and the Pharisees and the chief priests sent officers to take him" (John 7:31-32).

Jesus was often under the threat of death from the hatred of these wicked Pharisees. The Pharisees were men of great evil; but they should have been men of great goodness. Like I said, those who are offended, because they are corrected, turn into monsters. They become a variant that is very far from what they originally were.

Jesus answered them, I told you, and ye believed not: the works that I do in my Father's name, they bear witness of me. But ye believe not, because ye are not of my sheep, as I said unto you. My sheep hear my voice, and I know them, and they follow me: And I give unto them eternal life; and they shall never perish, neither shall any man pluck them out of my hand. My Father, which gave them me, is greater than all; and no man is able to pluck them out of my Father's hand. I and my Father are one. THEN THE JEWS

TOOK UP STONES AGAIN TO STONE HIM. JESUS ANSWERED THEM, MANY GOOD WORKS HAVE I SHEWED YOU FROM MY FATHER; FOR WHICH OF THOSE WORKS DO YE STONE ME?

John 10:25-32

Indeed, Jesus knew that the Pharisees and scribes were having several meetings to arrest and to kill Him. He asked them simply, "Why go ye about to kill me?" Why are you having meetings and trying to kill me? They hated Jesus Christ; but Jesus only spoke the truth to them.

Instead of turning into a monster, ask yourself whether the things that are being said are true or not. If the Pharisees had been honest in assessing the things Jesus was telling them, they would have come to the conclusion that they were only being told the truth.

Jesus answered them, and said, My doctrine is not mine, but his that sent me. If any man will do his will, he shall know of the doctrine, whether it be of God, or whether I speak of myself. He that speaketh of himself seeketh his own glory: but he that seeketh his glory that sent him, the same is true, and no unrighteousness is in him. Did not Moses give you the law, and yet none of you keepeth the law? WHY GO YE ABOUT TO KILL ME? The people answered and said, Thou hast a devil: who goeth about to kill thee?

John 7:16-20

4. King Joash the Monster

Joash was seven years old when he began to reign, and he reigned forty years in Jerusalem. His mother's name also was Zibiah of Beersheba. And Joash did that which was right in the sight of the LORD all the days of Jehoiada the priest. And Jehoiada took for him two wives; and he begat sons and daughters....

Now after the death of Jehoiada came the princes of Judah, and made obeisance to the king. Then the king hearkened unto them. And they left the house of the LORD God of their fathers, and served groves and idols: and wrath came upon Judah and Jerusalem for this their trespass. Yet he sent prophets to them, to bring them again unto the LORD; and they testified against them: but they would not give ear. AND THE SPIRIT OF GOD CAME UPON ZECHARIAH THE SON OF JEHOIADA THE PRIEST, WHICH STOOD ABOVE THE PEOPLE, AND SAID UNTO THEM, THUS SAITH GOD, WHY TRANSGRESS YE THE COMMANDMENTS OF THE LORD, THAT YE CANNOT PROSPER? BECAUSE YE HAVE FORSAKEN THE LORD, HE HATH ALSO FORSAKEN YOU. AND THEY CONSPIRED AGAINST HIM, AND STONED HIM WITH STONES AT THE COMMANDMENT OF THE KING IN THE COURT OF THE HOUSE OF THE LORD. Thus Joash the king remembered not the kindness which Jehoiada his father had done to him, but slew his son. And when he died, he said, The LORD look upon it, and require it.

2 Chronicles 24:1-3, 17-22

Joash, the king, is another example of someone who turned into a monster because he was corrected.

Joash was seven years old when he became the king. Jehoiada, the priest, looked after him and helped establish him as the king. Some years later, Jehoiada the priest died and his son, Zechariah who was also a priest, rebuked the king for going into idolatry. This angered Joash and he killed the son of the priest who had looked after him since he was seven years old.

Once again, a simple rebuke turned a good person into a monster.

CHAPTER 4

Offended:
Those Who Are Rejected

And he began to teach them, that the Son of man must suffer many things, and be rejected of the elders, and of the chief priests, and scribes, and be killed, and after three days rise again.

Mark 8:31

Those who are rejected become those who are offended! Rejection leads to offence. Rejection is a terrible experience that leaves a sore in your heart. Rejection is a sore in the heart and is caused by a feeling of "not really being a part of a group." Rejection is a feeling of being, somehow, on the outside and looking inside.

Seven Ways You Can be Rejected

1. Rejection can be caused by being part of a three-way fellowship. Anybody who has been part of a three-way friendship would have discovered that two of the three friends end up being closer, sharing secrets and sometimes ganging up against the one.

2. Rejection can happen when you are a foreigner from another country. This occurs when the majority is from the same country. A foreigner can, therefore more easily be hurt and develop a root of bitterness.

3. Rejection can happen when you have a different skin colour from the rest of the people. White people often feel rejected when black people are the majority and black people also feel rejected when they are in the minority.

4. Rejection can happen when you are less educated than the rest of the team. A lack of education, the lack of broadness and the lack of depth are things that soon manifest. Less educated people tend to be far more susceptible to feeling rejected than others.

5. Rejection can happen when you come from another tribe when everybody else comes from one particular tribe.

6. Rejection can happen when everyone else is a man and you are the only woman and vice-versa.

7. Rejection can happen when you are in the minority in anything. Minorities are more easily offended than the rest.

In my experience as a leader, people who feel rejected are difficult to please, no matter what you do for them. I remember a gentleman who had little or no qualifications. He was uneducated and did not know how deficient he really was. He lacked skills, he lacked broadness and he lacked depth. No matter what was done for him, he still felt rejected and unwanted!

CHAPTER 5

Offended:
Those Who Are Sacked

Then Adonijah the son of Haggith exalted himself, saying, I will be king: and he prepared him chariots and horsemen, and fifty men to run before him. And his father had not displeased him at any time in saying, Why hast thou done so? and he also was a very goodly man; and his mother bare him after Absalom. And he conferred with Joab the son of Zeruiah, and with Abiathar the priest: and they following Adonijah helped him. But Zadok the priest, and Benaiah the son of Jehoiada, and Nathan the prophet, and Shimei, and Rei, and the mighty men which belonged to David, were not with Adonijah.

1 Kings 1:5-8

Abiathar the priest was dismissed by Solomon because he helped Adonijah in the uprising that sought to make Adonijah the king instead of Solomon.

Abiathar had been a faithful priest throughout the reign of David and was of great help to King David in his fight against Absalom. There are many people who are like Abiathar. They have a long track record of being faithful; but even a longstanding and faithful person can do something that is deserving of dismissal. Always remember that the king by judgment establishes the land (Proverbs 29:4).

Solomon was forced to dismiss Abiathar for joining the rebellion that sought to enthrone Adonijah. He would have executed him if it were not for the fact that he had been to many battles with David and had carried the Ark of God.

Solomon did the right thing and dismissed Abiathar the priest.

Then to Abiathar the priest the king said, "Go to Anathoth to your own field, for you deserve to die; but I will not put you to death at this time, because you carried the ark of the Lord GOD before my father David, and because you were afflicted in everything with which my father was afflicted." SO SOLOMON DISMISSED ABIATHAR FROM BEING PRIEST TO THE LORD, in order to fulfill the word of the LORD, which He had spoken concerning the house of Eli in Shiloh.

1 Kings 2:26-27 (NASB)

Unfortunately, many longstanding employees, pastors and leaders do not take well to being dismissed.

I rarely dismiss people. But I have come to see that without dismissal it is impossible to gain control over the organisation that you lead. It is important that your dismissal is fair, just and equitable. It must not be too harsh and it must not be too lenient either. However in spite of doing what is right, you will always have people who react badly to being dismissed.

It is amazing to see how people react to dismissal. I remember a brother who had defiled a young lady. When he was rebuked, corrected and dismissed, his reaction was simply amazing. Instead of saying that he was sorry for his sins, he turned to the panel and rebuked them saying, "I am leaving you with a scar in my soul."

He continued, "All of you did not help me when I was going through my challenges and my difficulties. I had been expecting that you would reach out to me. No one contacted me and no one spoke to me." He went on to accuse them of spreading bad stories about him.

Indeed, that was an unfortunate and sad response to being dismissed. Instead of being repentant for defilement and committing immorality, this person was throwing accusations into the air. This is typical of people who are being dismissed.

I remember one administrator that I was forced to dismiss. This person was so angry at being sacked from full-time ministry. The response to being dismissed was to become disloyal and treacherous. Many people who are sacked become disloyal and treacherous. They hate you because you took a strong decision against them.

It is important to take strong decisions in the church and in the organisation that you lead. If you fail to take strong decisions to dismiss certain people, the organisation will fall apart.

The king by judgment establisheth the land: but he that receiveth gifts overthroweth it.

Proverbs 29:4

It is only by judgment that you can establish a church. When I look back at the short history of our church, it is the hard decisions that we took that have transformed the church into a worldwide ministry.

When you allow one centre of decay to continue in the same way, the rot and corruption spread out like a canker and defiles everything. Failing to discipline people is one of the greatest mistakes you can ever commit as a leader. Failing to sack and dismiss people when you have to, will be the undoing of your entire ministry.

CHAPTER 6

Offended: Those Who Are Offended by Greatness

Is not this the carpenter, the son of Mary, the brother of James, and Joses, and of Juda, and Simon? And are not his sisters here with us? And they were offended at him.

Mark 6:3

People who are close and familiar get offended when they have to receive you as a spiritual leader. "Who do you think you are?" is the question that is on the hearts of familiar people. In the days when Jesus walked the earth, His family had a hard time accepting Him as the Saviour of the world.

Today, we find it easier to receive from Jesus, Saviour of the world, because we did not grow up with Him or go to the same school with Him, neither do we know Jesus' relatives. It is therefore much easier for us to accept Him as the Saviour of the world. Unfortunately, when you are familiar with somebody, you struggle to see him as a gift from God.

People are offended with your greatness. It is dangerous to be great in this world.

Then Jesus answering said unto them, Go your way, and tell John what things ye have seen and heard; how that the blind see, the lame walk, the lepers are cleansed, the deaf hear, the dead are raised, to the poor the gospel is preached. And blessed is he, whosoever shall not be offended in me.

Luke 7:22-23

Your greatness may be due to your hard work. Your greatness may be due to your intelligence and great effort for many years. Solomon predicts that all the reward that a man will receive for his hard work is envy. Remember that Jesus Christ was killed because of envy! After doing all the right things, the reward from your fellow men is envy and jealousy.

Again, I considered all travail, and every right work, that for this a man is envied of his neighbour. This is also vanity and vexation of spirit.

Ecclesiastes 4:4

You will notice people speaking against great men whom they have never met. You will notice people having heated arguments about great men they do not know. They have only heard of them but have never had a chance to know them. There is spontaneous hatred for great people. There is an unprompted and inexplicable dislike for successful people. This is the offence that comes from greatness.

Decide that the greatness of someone will not spur you on to hatred but will inspire you to copy and to learn from those ahead of you. Never be jealous of a successful person. Never express dislike, distaste or disinterest in people who are successful.

Someone made a comment about holding evangelistic crusades. He said, "You can always gather a crowd in Africa or India, if you have enough money." As soon as he spoke those words, I knew that he was jealous of evangelists who had large crowds and gatherings. Instead of seeking to find how it was done, his dismissive remarks revealed his jealousy.

I heard another person say, "These large crowds are just to satisfy the ego of the foreign evangelist but it does not really get anyone saved." This is another statement from an envious pastor who failed to learn how to gather crowds.

I heard one other person say, "There is no need for larger and larger churches. I do not want to belong to a large church. A small church is much cosier and like a family."

Please do not join the jealous and envious losers of this life. Envious people speak out of their humiliation, their shame and their failure. Do not join them! You will never become something that you attack. You will never amount to much if you hate other people's greatness.

There is no doubt that people's greatness is offensive. The truth is that God is the One who lifts up one and puts down another. "For promotion cometh neither from the east, nor from the west, nor from the south. But God is the judge: he putteth down one, and setteth up another" (Psalm 75:6-7).

In the life of Solomon the king, we see God promising to give Solomon a level of greatness and success which would be unparalleled and unequalled for all time. Even though Solomon was very great, it was something that was given to him by the Lord. Why bother to be jealous, envious and offended about something that God has given to your neighbour? Fighting people who have been elevated by God will not help you.

Solomon Was Promised Greatness and Wealth by God

Wisdom and knowledge is granted unto thee; and I WILL GIVE THEE RICHES, and wealth, and honour, such as none of the kings have had that have been before thee, neither shall there any after thee have the like.

2 Chronicles 1:12

Solomon Receives Greatness and Wealth from God

And Solomon gathered chariots and horsemen: and he had a thousand and four hundred chariots, and twelve thousand horsemen, which he placed in the chariot cities, and with the king at Jerusalem. And THE KING MADE SILVER AND GOLD AT JERUSALEM AS PLENTEOUS AS STONES, and cedar trees made he as the sycomore trees that are in the vale for abundance. And Solomon had horses brought out of Egypt, and linen yarn: the king's merchants received the linen yarn at a price. And they fetched up, and brought forth out of Egypt a chariot for six hundred shekels of silver, and an horse for an hundred and fifty: and so brought they out horses for all the kings of the Hittites, and for the kings of Syria, by their means.

2 Chronicles 1:14-17

Money and wealth are very difficult to come by. No matter how hard you work, the ground yields very little. It truly takes a divine grace to come by abundance of a certain order. God gave this special abundance to Solomon. In the days of Solomon, silver became like stones that was lying on the ground outside. That is indeed a miracle!

There is no need to waste your emotions and to become envious, jealous or offended at something God Himself has done. Promotion does not come from the east or the west. The blessing of the Lord makes a person rich (Proverbs 10:22).

Do not be offended when God chooses to bless someone! The wealth of America irritates and offends many people. It would have been better for the wealth of America to stir up a desire in you to learn how they did it. You cannot learn from people you hate. You cannot truly benefit from someone you despise and have ill-will towards.

Abel Receives Promotion from God

And in process of time it came to pass, that Cain brought of the fruit of the ground an offering unto the LORD. And Abel, he also brought of the firstlings of his flock and of the fat thereof. And the LORD had respect unto Abel and to his offering: But unto Cain and to his offering he had not respect. And Cain was very wroth, and his countenance fell. And the LORD said unto Cain, Why art thou wroth? and why is thy countenance fallen? If thou doest well, shalt thou not be accepted? and if thou doest not well, sin lieth at the door. And unto thee shall be his desire, and thou shalt rule over him. And Cain talked with Abel his brother: and it came to pass, when they were in the field, that Cain rose up against Abel his brother, and slew him.

Genesis 4:3-8

Abel was honoured by God. God received his offering and rejected Cain's offering. Indeed, this offended Cain and turned him into an offended murderer. Do not allow someone else's promotion to turn you into an offended murderer.

Cain Is Offended

And in process of time it came to pass, that Cain brought of the fruit of the ground an offering unto the LORD. And Abel, he also brought of the firstlings of his flock and of the fat thereof. And the LORD had respect unto Abel and to his offering: But unto Cain and to his offering he had not respect. And Cain was very wroth, and his countenance fell. And the LORD said unto Cain, Why art thou wroth? and why is thy countenance fallen? If thou doest well, shalt thou not be accepted? and if thou doest not well, sin lieth at the door. And unto thee shall be his desire, and thou shalt rule over him. And Cain talked with Abel his brother: and it came to pass, when they were in the field, that Cain rose up against Abel his brother, and slew him.

Genesis 4:3-8

Why would you be offended because your brother goes higher in ministry? One day, a pastor visited us from outside the country. He confessed to something interesting at the end of his visit to our ministry. He said, "If I lived in Ghana, I think I would be jealous of you and hate you. I am glad I do not live in Ghana." Indeed, this man of God realised that God's promotion truly stirs up different sentiments in different people. Many times, your mere existence and success frightens, amazes and stirs up offence in the neighbour.

Jesus Was Promised Greatness

And, behold, thou shalt conceive in thy womb, and bring forth a son, and shalt call his name JESUS. HE SHALL BE GREAT, and shall be called the Son of the Highest: and the Lord God shall give unto him the throne of his father David: And he shall reign over the house of Jacob for ever; and of his kingdom there shall be no end.

Luke 1:31-33

Jesus Blessed Some and Offended Some

And Simeon blessed them, and said unto Mary his mother, Behold, this child is set for the fall and rising again of many in Israel; and for a sign which shall be spoken against;

Luke 2:34

Some people would be blessed by the greatness of Jesus Christ. Others would be offended at Jesus' greatness, His superiority and His glory. Are you going to be one of those who rise when you see the greatness of God's servant? Or are you going to be one of those who are offended at the greatness of God's servant? I warn you, do not let greatness offend you. God will bring you near greatness so that He can bless you and not destroy you.

The Greatness of Jesus Stirs up Offence

Then Jesus answering said unto them, Go your way, and tell John what things ye have seen and heard; how that the blind see, the lame walk, the lepers are cleansed, the deaf hear, the dead are raised, to the poor the gospel is preached. And BLESSED IS HE, WHOSOEVER SHALL NOT BE OFFENDED IN ME.

Luke 7:22-23

Indeed, the greatness of a person stirs up offence.

CHAPTER 7

Offended: Those Who Cannot Handle Hard Sayings

Then came his disciples, and said unto him, Knowest thou that the Pharisees were offended, after they heard this saying?

Matthew 15:12

Offended: Those Who Cannot Handle Hard Sayings

The Pharisees were constantly upset by Jesus' preaching, teachings and sayings. Jesus did not seek to please them in any way. They did not impress Him and He did not intend to humour them. Jesus was full of sharp rebukes for these double-timing pretenders clothed in religious clothes.

There are many people who are offended by what they are told. Their reaction is - "How dare you speak to me that way?" I remember an assistant pastor of a mega church who was greatly offended by his senior pastor's decision to transfer him from his headquarters to another city. This man of God visited our church and stood outside the gate of the church fuming about his senior pastor. "How dare he even mention the word 'transfer' in relation to me"? You see, this assistant pastor felt he was too big and too old in the church to be transferred away from the headquarters. The truth is that he was proud and puffed up. Indeed today, more than twenty years after this incident, this assistant pastor has amounted to nothing. He has not been able to pastor even the smallest church or build a tiny congregation.

Do not be put off by hard sayings! You must be tough and withstand rebukes, correction, reproof and any sharp words that are directed towards you. Paul told Timothy to use the scripture to rebuke, reproof and instruct people.

The word of God is not just praises and thanksgiving to you for your contribution to the ministry. We are not here to bow down to you and worship you because you sang a song or helped in the ushering today.

You are here to be corrected, rebuked and spoken to about any important thing that needs to be addressed. The reason why so many young girls marry without skills is because they are just told nice things all the time. Instead of being told to have their baths or learn how to cook, they are told that their hair is nice, their dress is nice, their shoes are beautiful and their face powder is excellent.

Once you have only the nice, soft sayings and words, you will be lopsided and will not develop well. Jesus said things that were hard to swallow. He told the people, "You will have to eat my flesh and drink my blood if you want to have eternal life" (John 6:51). Imagine telling people that they have to "eat my flesh and drink my blood." Should this offend them? It should not!

You must not allow yourself to be offended by any saying even if you do not understand it.

> **He that eateth my flesh, and drinketh my blood, dwelleth in me, and I in him. As the living Father hath sent me, and I live by the Father: so he that eateth me, even he shall live by me. This is that bread which came down from heaven: not as your fathers did eat manna, and are dead: he that eateth of this bread shall live for ever. These things said he in the synagogue, as he taught in Capernaum.**
>
> **Many therefore of his disciples, when they had heard this, said, THIS IS AN HARD SAYING; who can hear it? When Jesus knew in himself that his disciples murmured at it, he said unto them, DOTH THIS OFFEND YOU?**
>
> John 6:56-61

One day, a lady attended a church council meeting. There were many bishops there and she was questioned by other members of the panel on the use of some money that had been under her control. Thousands of dollars had been entrusted to her and she was expected to have built a church with the money. Somehow, the building was not constructed and the money was also missing.

The meeting that ensued was hot as they searched for the money. Amazingly, this lady was so offended by the questions that were asked about the missing money. Her attitude changed and though she had come into full-time ministry with zeal, she gradually became offended until she withdrew completely.

Her full-time ministry was short lived because offence was able to pick her out right at the beginning of her career in full-time ministry. As Jesus said, "Does this offend you?" Are you offended because I said you have to "eat my body and drink my blood"?

Do not let the fact that your boss raised his voice at you offend or disturb you. There are some bosses who raise their voices but mean well and are kind at heart. There are others who raise their voices and are simply murderers. You must choose to be among those who cannot be moved by hard or sharp sayings. You must toughen up so that you can withstand all forms of sayings. If you happened to be in a meeting where you were transferred to the battle front what would you do? You would have no choice but to receive the hard saying and move to the difficult battlefield as a good soldier. Endure hardness as a good soldier!

CHAPTER 8

Offended: Those Who Cannot Handle Trouble in the Leader's Life

And Jesus saith unto them, all ye shall be offended because of me this night: for it is written, I will smite the shepherd, and the sheep shall be scattered.

Mark 14:27

Whenever God's servants are attacked, there is a scattering and an offending of the sheep that takes place. It is important to overcome offences that occur in your life because of attacks on God's precious servants. Jesus predicted that people would be offended because of what would happen to Him on the night of His betrayal. If He was really such a good person, why would such things happen to Him?

Jesus knew that He was going to be struck down with the hatred of the Jews. Jesus Christ was going to be crucified. Everyone in town would see that Jesus had been crucified along with thieves. The masses would never know the truth. A common thief and a common criminal were the final verdict of the authorities who handled Jesus' case.

Jesus exited the city of Jerusalem on a cross. He was whipped and beaten like a scoundrel and a villain. Few people cared to know the real truth. No one really was ready to stand up to face the authorities and prevent the injustice from being meted out to Jesus Christ, Saviour of the world.

Whenever there is trouble in a leader's life, many people do not understand exactly what is happening. Some think he is guilty and some are confused. Many do not really care about what is happening.

For those who are real sticklers for righteousness, a leader's troubles can tip them away and make them turn against their own leader. At different stages of the ministry, I have had conflicts with different people and experienced crises after crises. Each time, I noticed the hearts of the people had these three responses - some were confused, others believed the stories, and others did not believe any bad thing about me.

One time, I was having meetings with some boys who were attacking the church. One of my church members made a comment behind my back but I heard about it. He said I was not taking my time to handle the issues. This fellow had no idea about how many meetings and negotiations I had had with these stubborn characters. When I heard those remarks, I smiled to myself because I knew an ignoramus had strayed into the fray and was making comments out of his empty head.

You will be surprised about how far from the truth the stories out there are. You will be amazed about the variant rumours that spread from talebearer to talebearer. Those who love you will never believe bad things about you.

Jesus said, "Tonight, you will be offended because of me" (John 14:27). Do not be offended because a man of God you love and admire is under fire. It is normal and expected for God's servants to go through fiery trials and temptations.

If you remember the book of Revelation, you will gain some understanding about what happens to God's servants as they serve Him. The dragon and the beast rose up to fight the church and the saints. Indeed, they were given power to blaspheme, insult and slander God's house. The blasphemies that were spoken by the beast were slander, detraction and speech that was injurious to another's good name. The blasphemy of the beast was the speaking of impious and reproachful words that were injurious to divine majesty. It is amazing that God allowed these beasts to have a chance to speak such terrible words against those that love God.

"And they worshipped the dragon which gave power unto the beast: and they worshipped the beast, saying, Who is like unto the beast? who is able to make war with him? And there was given unto him a mouth speaking great things and blasphemies; and power was given unto him to continue forty and two months. And he opened his mouth in blasphemy against God, to blaspheme his name, and his tabernacle, and them that dwell in heaven. And it was given unto him to make war with the saints, and to overcome them: and power was given him over all kindreds, and tongues, and nations" (Revelation 13:4-7).

Indeed, the dragon and the beast blasphemed, slandered and maligned God Himself. The dragon and the beast opened their mouth against God, God's name and God's tabernacle. They spoke blasphemies against all that dwelt in heaven. Truly, it seemed as though God's kingdom was defeated when the beast spoke endlessly against God and His kingdom.

Dear friend, this blasphemy was allowed for forty-two long months. At the end of the forty-two months, blasphemies were no longer allowed.

Dear friend, do not be put off by blasphemies and injurious speech levelled against God's man of faith and power.

The apostle Paul was in prison and died at the hands of cruel and unjust men. Paul died under the authority of Nero, one of the most depraved emperors of all time. Many people did not know who Paul was. Today, Paul is more famous than Nero. Today, Paul is more known than Nero.

Paul died as a common criminal; but there was one man called Onesiphorus who was not embarrassed by Paul's situation.

The Lord give mercy unto the house of Onesiphorus; for he oft refreshed me, AND WAS NOT ASHAMED OF MY CHAIN:

2 Timothy 1:16

Associating with Paul the prisoner, never embarrassed Onesiphorus. Are you like that? Are you happy to be associated with the messed-up reputation of God's servants or do you want to distance yourself from them because of the stories that are flying around about them? Are you embarrassed because of the bad reputation and blasphemies that are going around? Do not let that offend you!

The Bible that you read was written by many people who had bad reputations. The problems, scandals and failures of the men who wrote the Bible are not hidden from us. If you are looking for a perfect man with a perfect story line, you may have to stop reading the Bible. God loves His servants, no matter what men say about them.

Greatness must be sought in the eyes of God, not in the eyes of men. John the Baptist was destined to be great in the eyes of God and not in the eyes of men. That is what matters - greatness in the eyes of the Lord!

For he shall be great in the sight of the Lord, and shall drink neither wine nor strong drink; and he shall be filled with the Holy Ghost, even from his mother's womb.

Luke 1:15

CHAPTER 9

Offended: Those Who Are Abused

But WHOSO SHALL OFFEND ONE OF THESE LITTLE ONES which believe in me, it were better for him that a millstone were hanged about his neck, and that he were drowned in the depth of the sea. Woe unto the world because of offences! For it must needs be that offences come; but woe to that man by whom the offence cometh!

Matthew 18:6-7

To be abused is to be misused and mistreated unfairly. Abuse is usually done by someone who has power over you. This power over you may be because of his position, his authority or even his physical strength. Abuse of a person is a terrible experience.

By the time you come to your senses, a powerful person may have deceived you and cheated you of something you never intended to give away. Do not worry! God will judge anyone who has abused you. God is the avenger of such. It will be better that a millstone were hanged about their necks and drowned in the depths of the sea.

Abuse by authorities is one of the biggest sources of offence. Jesus said offending little ones and abusing little ones is a terrible mistake and a terrible sin. Jesus promised the most severe punishment to those who used their power to mislead, destroy and to cheat the little ones.

It is important to overcome this great source of offence called abuse. Abuse can set you off on a tangent. Abuse can destroy your foundations and change your personality. I have encountered people whose whole lives were changed because they were used and abused by a powerful authority figure who made them do their bidding. By the time they finished using these people, their lives were destroyed forever. If your life is destroyed by someone who abused you sexually or emotionally, you must press on towards healing and wholeness.

It is important to recognize that many people have been abused and misused in this life. Some people have recovered from this great offence. You must overcome too. You must be one of the people who overcame by the blood of the Lamb.

Do not allow satan's attempt to destroy your life to succeed! God will give you the upper hand in your personal and private crisis. It is important that you hold on to the scripture which says, "All things work together for good to them that love the Lord and who are the called according to his promise" (Romans 8:28).

The wounds of abuse that you have received will become scars lined with gold. The scars will be the basis of your healing ministry. Without scars, you will never have authority. The scars you have are evidence of wounds that have been healed. The scars you have are the evidence of what you have been through and what you have survived.

You have a choice before you. Either allow the works of satanic abuse perpetrated against you by wicked men to destroy you absolutely, or pick up from where you are and arise into the next post-abuse phase of your ministry.

CHAPTER 10

Offence: Weapon of Satan

To whom ye forgive any thing, I forgive also: for if I forgave any thing, to whom I forgave it, for your sakes forgave I it in the person of Christ; Lest Satan should get an advantage of us: for we are not ignorant of his devices.

2 Corinthians 2:10-11

Offence and unforgiveness are satan's great weapons against the church.

Once I was offended greatly by the government of my country because they attacked our church and destroyed our building illegally. A senior minister who advised me at the time warned me about becoming offended. He said, "Do not allow this to change you. If you allow hurt to grow in you, it will change you and change your message. Instead of preaching Christ, you will preach your wounds."

Indeed, hurt and offended people only preach and speak from their wounds and hurts. Offence changes a person almost like salvation changes a person. Offence is something that happens when satan has targeted you for destruction and elimination.

Offence is a great weapon of satan against the church. Every person must set himself in readiness to be hurt one day. Once you are offended, a great plan to destroy you has been set in motion.

Do not take the subject of offence lightly. Offence will remove you from the race when nothing else works against you. Do not also think you cannot be taken down by any of the enemy's tricks. Indeed, satan's mature plan against you is to make you offended.

I once read a story about satan's plans to destroy some Christians. In the story, satan was getting rid of some out-dated items, gadgets and equipment. He organized a sale of many of the items in his arsenal. Indeed, satan wanted to raise some funds to finance his campaign. The equipment on sale were things like alcoholism, drug addiction, depravities, incest, witchcraft and lying.

However, there were two items which were not on sale at all: offence and fornication. So someone asked satan why he was not selling those two items. Satan answered that those two gadgets were his best items. He always had a hundred per cent success rate when he used them (offence and fornication). No matter how out-dated and frivolous they seemed, they always worked. Satan explained that these pieces of equipment (offence and fornication) were of international quality and worked, irrespective of country, race, tribe, colour language or age.

Woe unto the world because of offences! For it must needs be that offences come; but woe to that man by whom the offence cometh!

Matthew 18:7

Offence is guaranteed to appear in your life at some point in time. It is a successful weapon in satan's arsenal. Offence works well on those who have survived other attacks. However offence does not work on those who are alerted and prepared for it.

Many years ago, a pastor made a comment to me. He said God had showed him the importance of having a sweet spirit all the time. What the pastor was actually saying was that he needed to guard against ever allowing offence to settle in his heart.

Once offence has settled in your heart, you will not have a sweet spirit and you will change.

The changes you go through when offended are a terrible metamorphosis into an unrecognizable monster of evil. When you eventually recover from your hurts and look back you will be surprised at what you became when you were hurt.

Being hurt is one of the greatest spiritual attacks you will ever experience. Don't take the subject of offence lightly because Jesus predicted that you would be offended by all means.

Learn the principles and understand the schemes that are behind you being hurt.

Do you know when you will realize you are simply an offended person who couldn't cope with offences? You will realize this when you have turned into a caricature of yourself - so far from what you once were.

When you become demonized, far gone into the deep end of evil, you will see that satan actually fooled you and led you to become the exact opposite of what you have ever believed. To your own amazement, your hurts will turn you into a betrayer of all that you have ever believed.

And then shall many be offended, and shall betray one another, and shall hate one another.
Matthew 24:10

Indeed there are stages in becoming offended. Offence is something that grows on you. Like the stages in becoming disloyal, you don't realize what is happening to you until you become Judas Iscariot himself. What are the stages you go through when offended? There are seven stages that an offended person goes through;

Stages of Offence

1. Withdrawal

2. Resentment, hatred

3. Mistrust

4. Malice and ill-will

5. Stubbornness

6. Treachery, betrayal

7. Demonization

CHAPTER 11

Stage of Offence: Withdrawal

I sleep, but my heart waketh: it is the voice of my beloved that knocketh, saying, Open to me, my sister, my love, my dove, my undefiled: for my head is filled with dew, and my locks with the drops of the night. I have put off my coat; how shall I put it on? I have washed my feet; how shall I defile them? My beloved put in his hand by the hole of the door, and my bowels were moved for him. I rose up to open to my beloved; and my hands dropped with myrrh, and my fingers with sweet smelling myrrh, upon the handles of the lock. I opened to my beloved; but my beloved had withdrawn himself, and was gone: my soul failed when he spake: I sought him, but I could not find him; I called him, but he gave me no answer.

Song of Songs 5:2-6

Stage of Offence: Withdrawal

Withdrawal is a reflex action that happens very naturally. From the scripture above we see beloveds making overtures acts towards each other. However, one of them seemed reluctant to respond to the love. When he eventually did, his lover was gone. Withdrawn! Moved away!

Indeed that is the story of love spurned and love that is hurt. Little things can hurt lovers. It is because there was great love that there is great hurt. Things afar off do not hurt you; but things really close to your heart are hurtful.

The reluctance, the delays and the seeming disinterest in expressing love caused the withdrawal. Withdrawal is the first stage of offence and can be more easily overcome than other stages.

1. WITHDRAWAL IS THE FIRST STAGE OF THE SYNDROME OF OFFENCE.

Offence naturally makes you withdraw yourself from what hurts or strikes you. Would you go towards a stick that is hitting you or would you withdraw from it? It is a natural reflex to pull back from the offending strike.

Offended people are always withdrawn. Watch out for this all-important sign of offence. It is the beginning of great waters flowing against you. Withdrawal is the beginning of a big flood against the offended person.

You will not and cannot imagine what will come out of the offended person. There are several ways in which withdrawal takes place. Withdrawal basically takes place when a person withdraws from relationships. The more important and close the relationship, the more serious the implications of withdrawal.

2. WITHDRAWAL IS WORSE THAN IF YOU MAINTAINED RELATIONSHIPS.

Two are better than one; because they have a good reward for their labour. For if they fall, the one will lift up his fellow: but woe to him that is alone when he falleth; for he hath not another to help him up. Again, if two lie together, then they have heat: but how can one be warm alone? And if one prevail against him, two shall withstand him; and a threefold cord is not quickly broken.

Ecclesiastes 4:9-12

Why do you think two are better than one? Yes, you can survive on your own! But two are better than one. It is a law. The relationship is better than no relationship. If you break the law the law will break your life. This famous scripture about two being better than one is revealing the importance of relationships and why you should not withdraw from any relationship. There are problems in relationships but there are even greater problems arising from isolation and withdrawal.

Withdrawal reduces the impact of your ministry. Your reward is not the same any longer.

Withdrawal prevents and blocks the help you could ever receive from anyone. If someone would have lifted you up, he will no longer do so. You will stay down because you withdrew from an important relationship.

Withdrawal prevents you from properly defending yourself.

Offended people withdraw from their best friends. Your ability to maintain friendships and relationships is a revelation of how you have not allowed the spirit of offence to enter your life. Indeed, you must take recognition of how long you have maintained relationships with people. If you have many people with whom you don't flow anymore it reveals that offence is really working in your life. There are pastors who used to be great friends but do not relate anymore.

Offended people withdraw from relationships at church.

Offended people leave churches.

Offended pastors resign from churches.

Offended Christians withdraw from church friendships. Instead of flowing, chatting and relating happily, they slink away, making no comment about anything anymore. Watch out for the withdrawn person! He is offended and unless he is healed, there are going to be more developments from him or her.

Offended people withdraw from pastoral relationships. The person they used to call their pastor is now a source of offence. How does this happen?

3. WITHDRAWAL CUTS ESSENTIAL SUPPLIES THAT YOU NEED.

> But speaking the truth in love, we are to grow up in all aspects into Him who is the head, even Christ, from whom the whole body, being fitted and held together by what every joint supplies, according to the proper working of each individual part, causes the growth of the body for the building up of itself in love.
>
> Ephesians 4:15-16 (NASB)

Withdrawal is the first thing that happens to weaken the offended person. Relationships are the greatest source of inputs and strength for a believer. When you withdraw, you cut yourself off from your source of power, strength and wisdom. Notice how God considers our relationships as a source of supply. You are who you are by the supplies that come from every joint in your life.

When relationships created by God to bless and strengthen you are destroyed, your weaknesses and hollowness will soon be revealed. When people leave churches, they become ghosts and phantoms of what they were called to be. They were destined for greatness but crashed to the ground because they cut themselves off from their blessings, strengths and supplies.

Many wars were lost because the supplies to the soldiers did not reach them. If you send one million soldiers to war, you must have supplies for these men. They will be hungry every day!

They will be thirsty every day! They will be sick every day! You will need to supply all their needs every day!

When Hitler sent out millions of soldiers to attack the Soviet Union, he had to supply them with food and clothing to keep them alive. In the end, the distances involved and the difficulties on the ground made it impossible to continue sending supplies. Many of the soldiers perished from cold and hunger. They were soundly defeated because they lacked the necessary supplies to survive the winter in Russia.

Do you want to be soundly defeated in battle? If you want to survive your battles you must stay connected and maintain the supplies of wisdom, guidance and counsel God has given you. Maintain your essential relationships! Do not cut off the very pipeline that supplies you with water.

4. TO WITHDRAW IS TO MAKE A VERY BASIC MISTAKE OF CHRISTIANITY.

Let us hold unswervingly to the hope we profess, for he who promised is faithful. And let us consider how we may spur one another on toward love and good deeds, not giving up meeting together, as some are in the habit of doing, but encouraging one another - and all the more as you see the Day approaching.

Hebrews 10:23-25 (NIV)

To withdraw is to make a very basic mistake in your Christian life. Scripture enjoins us to fight to fellowship and meet together so that we can encourage one another.

Withdrawing is a basic mistake because it takes away the root of fellowship. Fellowshipping and relating is basic to Christianity. We get stronger every time we meet together.

They go from strength to strength, every one of them in Zion appeareth before God.

Psalm 84:7

Stage of Offence: Withdrawal

Each step you take in withdrawal is to move you from weakness to weakness. Withdrawal is the opposite of fellowship. That is why the devil's first suggestion is that you withdraw from fellowship.

5. WITHDRAWAL FROM RELATIONSHIPS REVEALS YOU ARE DIVORCE- PRONE.

But if you do marry, you have not sinned; and if a virgin marries, she has not sinned. But those who marry will face many troubles in this life, and I want to spare you this.

1 Corinthians 7:28 (NIV)

Paul promised married couples many troubles, storms and difficulties. Where do these come from? They come from the human nature that is pride-filled and contention-prone.

Only by pride cometh contention: but with the well advised is wisdom.

Proverbs 13:10

There are many problems in human relationships. Marriage is the best place to see the many problems that exist in human relationships. Many hurt couples that are wounded beyond recovery are the evidence of this reality. If you cannot maintain a good relationship with a brother who does not live with you or depend on you then it's not likely you will have a good and peaceful marriage either.

Many people move away from relationships because they are divorce-prone. Anyone who can suddenly and abruptly stop relating with someone they have been close to for many years reveals that they are likely to break other love relationships.

It is important to look at the relationships a person has been able to maintain for many years.

If you can withdraw from someone so important to your life as your mother or father, then who can you not separate from in the future?

6. WITHDRAWAL CUTS YOU OFF FROM "KOINONIA".

> Then they that gladly received his word were baptized: and the same day there were added unto them about three thousand souls. And they continued stedfastly in the apostles' doctrine and fellowship, and in breaking of bread, and in prayers. And fear came upon every soul: and many wonders and signs were done by the apostles.
>
> Acts 2:41-43

The scripture above shows us that the disciples continued in fellowship. They did not stop fellowshipping after the initial experience of the Holy Ghost. By refusing to withdraw they had the *"koinonia"* of the apostles and brethren. *"Koinonia"* is a Greek word with amazing revelations and meanings.

"Koinonia" speaks of partnership. Withdrawal cuts you off from partnerships that are essential for your success.

"Koinonia" speaks of participation. Withdrawal cuts you off from participation of important people in your life that are essential for your success.

"Koinonia" speaks of intercourse. Withdrawal cuts you off from intercourse or very deep relationships that are essential for your success in life and ministry. Indeed, there are some very deep relationships God will give you for your benefit. Indeed, the deeper the relationship the more fruit you bear.

"Koinonia" speaks of communion. Withdrawal cuts you off from communion that you need in your life.

"Koinonia" speaks of contribution. Withdrawal cuts you off from the contribution that someone has to make in your life.

CHAPTER 12

Stage of Offence: Resentment

Looking diligently lest any man fail of the grace of God; lest any root of bitterness springing up trouble you, and thereby many be defiled;

Hebrews 12:15

Resentment is a feeling of bitterness and anger. It is the persisting ill-will that you have towards someone because you feel they have wronged you. Resentment is indeed a dangerous feeling to have.

Resentment is a "root of bitterness". A "root" is the basic source, cause and origin of something.

Resentment and bitterness are the basic causes of the evil that comes from an offended person. It festers and it grows from below until it dominates you.

You can understand the six powerful effects of a root of bitterness by understanding the six functions of a natural root system.

The functions of root are as follows:

1. A root is basically an anchor of the plant to the soil. A root of bitterness anchors hatred and gives it a platform to work from.

2. A root system is used to absorb water and nutrients from the soil. A root of bitterness absorbs more complaints and evils into the heart of the offended person.

3. A root conducts absorbed water and nutrients to the stem. A root of bitterness conducts and transfers bitterness and wickedness into every part of the person. The bitterness and malice move from the head to the heart and to the body resulting in outward manifestations of wickedness. Bitter Christians are plagued with illnesses and disease.

4. A root is a storehouse of food. Roots, like yam tubers, are storehouses of food. A root of bitterness is a storehouse of evil intent and unforgiveness. When a root of bitterness exists, it is a storehouse of unhappiness and sadness. When you go to a person with a root of bitterness you encounter a full storeroom of ill intent and malice.

Stage of Offence: Resentment

5. Roots are used for vegetative reproduction and to overcome competition with other plants. The root of bitterness is the basis for competition and reproduction of evil. Roots of bitterness are the reasons for jealousy, envy and fighting that never ends.

CHAPTER 13

Stage of Offence: Mistrust and Suspicion

And there was a very sore battle that day; and Abner was beaten, and the men of Israel, before the servants of David. And there were three sons of Zeruiah there, Joab, and Abishai, and Asahel: and Asahel was as light of foot as a wild roe. And Asahel pursued after Abner; and in going he turned not to the right hand nor to the left from following Abner. Then Abner looked behind him, and said, Art thou Asahel? And he answered, I am. And Abner said to him, Turn thee aside to thy right hand or to thy left, and lay thee hold on one of the young men, and take thee his armour. But Asahel would not turn aside from following of him. And Abner said again to Asahel, Turn thee aside from following me: wherefore should I smite thee to the ground? how then should I hold up my face to Joab thy brother? Howbeit he refused to turn aside: wherefore Abner with the hinder end of the spear smote him under the fifth rib, that the spear came out behind him; and he fell down there, and died in the same place: and it came to pass, that as many as came to the place where Asahel fell down and died stood still.

2 Samuel 2:17-23

And Abner had communication with the elders of Israel, saying,

Ye sought for David in times past to be king over you: Now then do it: for the Lord hath spoken of David, saying, By the hand of my servant David I will save my people Israel out of the hand of the Philistines, and out of the hand of all their enemies. And Abner also spake in the ears of Benjamin: and Abner went also to speak in the ears of David in Hebron all that seemed good to Israel, and that seemed good to the whole house of Benjamin. So Abner came to David to Hebron, and twenty men with him.

And David made Abner and the men that were with him a feast. And Abner said unto David, I will arise and go, and will gather all Israel unto my lord the king, that they may make a league with thee, and that thou mayest reign over all that thine heart desireth. And David sent Abner away; and he went in peace. And, behold, the servants of David and Joab came from pursuing a troop, and brought in a great spoil with them: but Abner was not with David in Hebron; for he had sent him away, and he was gone in peace.

When Joab and all the host that was with him were come, they told Joab, saying, Abner the son of Ner came to the king, and he hath sent him away, and he is gone in peace. Then Joab came to the king, and said, What hast thou done? Behold, Abner came unto thee; why is it that thou hast sent him away, and he is quite gone? Thou knowest Abner the son of Ner, that he came to deceive thee, and to know thy going out and thy coming in, and to know all that thou doest.

And when Joab was come out from David, he sent messengers after Abner, which brought him again from the well of Sirah: but David knew it not. And when Abner was returned to Hebron, Joab took him aside in the gate to speak with him quietly, and smote him there under the fifth rib, that he died, for the blood of Asahel his brother. And afterward when David heard it, he said, I and my kingdom are guiltless before the Lord for ever from the blood of Abner the son of Ner:

2 Samuel 3:17-28

Joab, the commander of David's army had suffered a terrible blow when his brother Asahel was killed by Abner. This terrible experience had wounded and offended Joab. When Joab found out who killed his brother he vowed to revenge. Joab would never trust Abner as long as he lived. A wounded and offended person is a suspicious and untrusting person.

Joab did not trust Abner's overtures of friendship. Why? Abner was offended when Joab killed his brother. He could not bring himself to trust Abner's attempt to befriend the camp of David.

This is what Joab said about Abner, "Thou knowest Abner the son of Ner, that he came to deceive thee, and to know thy going out and thy coming in, and to know all that thou doest" (2 Samuel 3:25). Indeed, this scripture shows that Joab had no trust for Abner.

An offended person is distrustful. Are you trusting or are you generally suspicious? Often, a man or woman who is generally suspicious and untrusting, has been offended by someone in the past.

Do not expect someone who is offended to ever really trust you. Indeed, all your efforts at loving people who are offended may be like pouring water into a toilet bowl. (When water is poured into a toilet bowl, it never gets full).

There are many examples of untrusting. offended people. For instance, if a man has experienced treachery and betrayal before, he has been wounded by the acts of disloyalty. Such a person would not be trusting of people who give speeches declaring their loyalty.

Once I gave someone a gift. This person who received the gift was full of appreciation and came to me pouring out many words of appreciation. But to everyone's surprise I stopped him in his tracks. I said, "These words are offensive to me. It reminds me of your betrayal of me."

This particular person had been very good at saying "Thank you" in the past but had been discovered saying many negative things behind my back as well. I had learnt the hard way that profuse thanks and shows of appreciation did not mean the person was loyal and faithful. "Stop it!" I exclaimed. I stopped the person in the middle of saying "Thank you" because I was offended by his disloyalty and treachery.

An offended person is indeed an untrusting and suspicious individual. I once met a woman who had seen her friends mistreated by boys. She could narrate at length and in detail how each of her friends was badly treated by their boyfriends. She knew how each girl's heart was broken by each relationship. She virtually relived each case of infidelity against her friends. The unfaithful and treacherous behaviour of boys greatly offended this young girl's sensitivities.

Indeed, this wound was so deep that she could not get married. Man after man came her way proposing love. She was a very beautiful girl and had many suitors. Somehow, she never trusted any of them. Even though she had over twenty potential suitors, she rejected all of them and remained unmarried till her death. Indeed, she had been wounded in her soul by watching other girls suffer heartbreaks. She could never bring herself to trust men as long as she lived.

It is not nice to love a suspicious and untrusting person. You can give the whole world to the person but they will still not trust you. You can cut off your head and give it to the person on a plate and the person will still not believe in your love. Even the smiles of a distrustful person glimmer with suspicion. All your kindness to such a person is a waste of time. They will never like you from their heart because they are offended.

Indeed, the root of bitterness is a terrible and destructive seed. It even destroys a person's ability to receive love!

CHAPTER 14

Stage of Offence: Malice, Ill-Will

For we ourselves also were sometimes foolish, disobedient, deceived, serving divers lusts and pleasures, LIVING IN MALICE AND ENVY, HATEFUL, AND HATING ONE ANOTHER.

Titus 3:3

Paul describes his life in the past as being full of malice, envy and hate! Indeed, that is the lot of most people in this world. Malice, ill-will, hatred and wickedness! People are filled with these evil vices before Christ saves them. Salvation removes these things from the heart of a believer. After salvation, your heart is filled with the love of God instead of hate, malice and ill-will. Indeed, your new feelings of love are a sign of your salvation.

> For this is the message that ye heard from the beginning, that we should love one another. Not as Cain, who was of that wicked one, and slew his brother. And wherefore slew he him? Because his own works were evil, and his brother's righteous. Marvel not, my brethren, if the world hate you. We know that we have passed from death unto life, because we love the brethren. He that loveth not his brother abideth in death.
>
> 1 John 3:11-14

So how does a believer get into malice and ill-will if these things are removed from our heart at salvation?

Indeed, believers also get filled with these evil things when they are offended.

I remember a brother who was offended when he was disciplined in the ministry. He went about saying many things with the intent of harming the church and I. He wanted to prevent people from supporting me and giving to the ministry.

He spread stories and reported me to various authorities so that they would investigate me. I marvelled at the evil intent that this fellow had towards me. At a point one could feel that they would kill you if they had a chance to.

> Thou hast seen all their vengeance and all their imaginations against me. Thou hast heard their reproach, O Lord, and all their imaginations against me; The lips of those that rose up against me, and their device against me

all the day. Behold their sitting down, and their rising up; I am their musick. Render unto them a recompence, O Lord, according to the work of their hands. Give them sorrow of heart, thy curse unto them.

Lamentations 3:60-65

Malice and ill-will is a terrible stage in the development of offence! Jeremiah experienced the withering hatred and ill-will of people he had ministered to.

He described them as people who devised things against him all the day long. Malice is the desire to inflict injury, harm, or suffering on someone.

The people Jeremiah was dealing with were filled with malice towards him. They wanted something bad to happen to Jeremiah. Jeremiah ended up cursing them for their persistent ill-will and malice towards him.

The person you have these hostile impulses towards is the person you blame for your humiliation. When someone offends you, a deep-seated meanness and ill-will grows in you towards the person.

Many people who develop malice and ill-will have not taken correction and rebukes well. They are so slighted by the confrontation that they go off the deep end and nurture wickedness in their hearts towards the person they believe has offended them.

I once found out that one of my pastors was harbouring hatred and ill-will towards me. He had predicted my downfall to his friend. Indeed, he predicted my downfall several times to this friend. He harboured a deep-seated resentment towards me.

I once rebuked, corrected and counselled a pastor. I found out fifteen years later that this person was full of hatred for me and had lived fifteen years harbouring malice and ill-will towards me. Even on occasions when I would show this person great love, he would interpret it differently and castigate me behind my back for my very act of love and giving.

It's amazing that a wounded person is like a wounded animal. Any attempt to go near, even to show love is useless. A wounded animal is more dangerous and will kill the very person who is out to help it. So it is with wounded and hurt people. They are filled with the desire to harm, hurt, strike back, or inflict some kind of evil on even the person who shows them kindness.

I once overheard someone advising his friend. He said, "When you see a snake on the road, don't drive over it. Don't drive over it to kill it," he warned. I wondered why! He continued, "When a snake is driven over, it may not die but be injured; and it may be caught up in the tires of the car and come up into the car. Then this wounded snake would become even more dangerous and would attack anything that moves near it. You would be in even greater danger because you are near a malicious, wounded, evil snake."

Indeed, you need to be careful with wounded people. It's as though their minds don't work properly anymore. They are filled with malice and ill-will. They are bent on harming you.

That's why Paul said that we should put aside malice and ill-will. The whole world is full of seven billion offended people who are filled with malice and ill-will towards one another. Indeed that is why every country needs the police, the courts, judges and an army.

If human beings are let loose on one another, they will be at each other's throat in no time. Each one will blame the other for his failure.

Offended people are usually failures. They are looking for someone to blame for their failure, humiliation and shame in this life. Malicious people want to exact their revenge on you for something that is their own fault.

Cain was a failure! Cain was humiliated by God's rejection of his offering. How did he respond? By developing a malevolent and hateful attitude towards his brother. He wanted to revenge on his brother for something that had nothing to do with his brother Abel.

> And in process of time it came to pass, that Cain brought of the fruit of the ground an offering unto the Lord. And Abel, he also brought of the firstlings of his flock and of the fat thereof. And the Lord had respect unto Abel and to his offering: But unto Cain and to his offering he had not respect. And Cain was very wroth, and his countenance fell. And the Lord said unto Cain, Why art thou wroth? and why is thy countenance fallen? If thou doest well, shalt thou not be accepted? and if thou doest not well, sin lieth at the door. And unto thee shall be his desire, and thou shalt rule over him. And Cain talked with Abel his brother: and it came to pass, when they were in the field, that Cain rose up against Abel his brother, and slew him.
>
> Genesis 4:3-8

Such people want to attack the softest target they can find. They want to inflict on it the maximum damage. Someone once said to me, "When this person speaks about you it's damaging, malicious and spiteful." Why would someone spend his time damaging me spitefully? What have I done to the person? Indeed, you do not need to harm anyone to experience the spitefulness of humanity. Indeed, people you love can really be malicious to you as their way of saying "Thank you."

CHAPTER 15

Stage of Offence: Stubbornness

A brother offended is harder to win than a strong city...

Proverbs 18:19 (NKJV)

This scripture means that it is a lot easier to conquer or win a strong city than reconcile a brother who is offended.

The next stage of offence is stubbornness. A person becomes stubborn when he feels that he is right and has been wronged. A hardening takes place in the person's soul.

Offended people have a very good memory for bad things that have happened to them but a poor memory for the good things that have been done for them. This selective memory for bad things helps them always remember wrongs committed against them. It is this selective memory that is the basis for the stubbornness that is found in an offended person.

The painful memories become a mental picture they permanently carry around. This is a major blessing blocker.

The scripture says that a brother offended is harder to be won than capturing a fenced city.

Offended people rarely change their minds. I remember one offended person who was rebuked and corrected about a minor issue. This individual became so offended that nothing could change his mind for fifteen years. Over the period of fifteen years every possible act of love was shown to this person. Yet, in stubbornness, this individual refused to see anything good in anything that was ever done. Watch out for those who are hard and stubborn. They are probably wounded soldiers.

Stubbornness is always a bad sign! Stubbornness is like jaundice! Jaundice is the yellowing of the eyes or lips of an individual. Jaundice is always a bad thing whether in a child or in an adult. There is no type of jaundice that doesn't mean something bad. Sometimes jaundice means sickle cell disease. Sometimes jaundice means hepatitis or liver infections. Sometimes jaundice means cancer is developing. Jaundice always has a bad meaning whatever the cause.

Stubbornness is like jaundice! It always has a bad meaning whenever you see it. Stubbornness can be caused by a bad trait in a child! In the Bible such stubborn children were even to be put to death.

> If a man have a stubborn and rebellious son, which will not obey the voice of his father, or the voice of his mother, and that, when they have chastened him, will not hearken unto them: Then shall his father and his mother lay hold on him, and bring him out unto the elders of his city, and unto the gate of his place; And they shall say unto the elders of his city, This our son is stubborn and rebellious, he will not obey our voice; he is a glutton, and a drunkard. And all the men of his city shall stone him with stones, that he die: so shalt thou put evil away from among you; and all Israel shall hear, and fear.
>
> Deuteronomy 21:18-21

Stubbornness is associated with rebellion and witchcraft.

> For rebellion is as the sin of witchcraft, and stubbornness is as iniquity and idolatry. Because thou hast rejected the word of the Lord, he hath also rejected thee from being king.
>
> 1 Samuel 15:23

Stubbornness is something that is found in offended people. Like I said, stubbornness, like jaundice, is always a bad thing. It is always a bad sign. "A brother offended is harder to win than a strong city" (Proverbs 18:19, NKJV). This means that it is a lot easier to conquer or win a strong city than to reconcile with a brother who is offended.

CHAPTER 16

Stage of Offence: Treachery

And then many will be offended, will betray one another, and will hate one another.

Matthew 24:10

Treachery is the act of betrayal! When you practice treachery against your country it is called treason. A traitor is someone who betrays you! A traitor is someone who betrays the trust you reposed in him.

Offended people become traitors as part of their manifestations.

There are seven ways in which an offended person manifests in the stage of treachery.

Signs of a Traitor

1. An offended traitor will deliver or expose anything he can to an enemy.

2. An offended traitor will be unfaithful in guarding secrets entrusted to him.

3. An offended traitor will disappoint your hopes and expectations greatly.

4. An offended traitor will reveal something you would prefer to conceal.

5. An offended traitor will deceive you in any way he can.

6. An offended traitor will disclose secrets in violation of the oath taken.

7. An offended traitor corrupts those around him. Usually, a traitor turns the people around him into traitors too.

When you relate with people, always look twice at them and imagine what it would be like if that person betrayed you. What would it be like if that person one day turned against you? What would it be like if that person goes away and re-describes his friendship and relationship with you?

I remember an offended brother who constantly gave information about me to an enemy. Unknown to me, this person was so offended that he secretly gave away information about me. Little did I know that I was under constant surveillance!

My movements and travels were monitored and even what I ate was under discussion by an enemy. It's amazing that offence can turn a really nice and good person into a traitor.

Never become a traitor in all your life. Jesus said it would have been better if Judas had not been born (Matthew 26:24).

Benedict Arnold is the most famous traitor of the United States because he betrayed his country. When he defected to the British side, he was given a high position in the British army. However, the British soldiers did not yield and respond to his leadership as expected. They were offended that Benedict Arnold would be made an officer over them.

A traitor is a traitor whether he is in your side or not. No one wants or likes a traitor. Traitors are always treated as demons. It is a horrible thing to become a traitor. Traitors are executed at the next opportunity!

Try with all your might to never descend into the abyss and become a traitor. No one ever calls his child "Judas" anymore. A traitor is synonymous with a devil! Being a traitor is like being a human devil! No one can trust you anymore!

A traitor is someone who is highly trusted but lets down the one who trusted him.

To discover that someone has disclosed things about you that you would rather keep private is an ultimate blow!

When you lose trust you will sweat for the rest of your life to gain what was once handed to you on a silver platter.

Don't become a Judas because of your hurts; don't become a Benedict Arnold because of your hurts, or even the devil will not trust you when you apply to work for him!

CHAPTER 17

Stage of Offence: Demonization

Then entered Satan into Judas surnamed Iscariot, being of the number of the twelve. And he went his way, and communed with the chief priests and captains, how he might betray him unto them.

Luke 22:3-4

Judas was not demonized when Jesus appointed him to the high office of ministry. Judas was given an opportunity very few people will ever get. None of us will ever get the chance to be one of the twelve apostles. Judas threw all that away because he allowed an evil spirit to lead him to do the unthinkable and the unreasonable!

Jesus had proved over and over again that He was the Son of God. Judas had watched Jesus raise the dead and perform astounding miracles. To turn against this supernatural figure you have been with for three years made no sense at all. What would thirty pieces of silver do for anyone? It could only buy a plot of land. Yet for this paltry sum of money, Judas ended his stay in the ministry.

There is no doubt that people who are offended become demonized. The evidence that people are demonized is found in the unreasonable things that they do. The presence of a demon is always revealed by unreasonable and irrational behaviour.

Judas' actions reveal a madness that is commonly seen in offended people who are in the last stages of their insanity. Absolute madness characterizes the behaviour of a hurt and offended person.

People become demonized at the end of their lives and at the end of the road of offence. The madness is fuelled by their humiliation, their failure, their shame and their mad desire for revenge at all costs.

When someone acts completely out of sync with reason, you must always suspect demons. I once encountered a minister who believed strongly in my ministry and claimed that everything he had ever learnt came from me. This minister was also ordained and appointed by me into the highest levels of ministry. He tried to start a church on his own but in the process he fell to demons and evil spirits.

The reason I say this is because the things he said did not make sense. Why attack the person who appointed you, trained you and ordained you into ministry? Why say that the person who you called father for fifteen years is now satan? Why insult openly the one who ordained you? How would you establish any kind of authority yourself?

This same fellow was known to speak highly of me and give me much honour. One day he said to a son of mine that he felt that his ministry was just to be close to me. Indeed, this young man launched a vengeful and hate filled attack on my person and against all reason and the principles that he had espoused for many years.

I sat in amazement and watched this man set fire to his own hair. Only demons could make a person do the things he was doing to himself. Indeed he felt he was harming me but actually, he was harming himself and setting fire to his own body.

How did all this happen? It happened when this man was corrected and asked to step in line. He was no longer allowed to do his own thing. His anger and hurt at being corrected was phenomenal.

The Dream

I remember a story I read about a pastor who was in contention with another minister in the same church. There was deep strife and offence between these ministers. As the brother lay in bed God opened his eyes and he beheld a huge evil spirit standing in the room.

This fierce demon spirit was standing upright wearing armour. The man could see each piece of armour and understand it's symbolic meaning.

The fierce evil spirit wore a helmet of pride!

The evil spirit wore a breastplate of unrighteousness!

The demon creature carried a sword of bitterness!

The demon creature also had a shield of hatred!

There was a hammer of revenge hanging from the belt of the demon creature.

The evil spirit wore a large cloak of deception!

The feet of this evil creature were shod with boots of anger!

God spoke to the man and said to him, look at what you have allowed into your room and into your heart. Your ministry will be destroyed by the presence of this evil creature you have opened the door to.

Indeed, all the items in the armour of this evil spirit are present in the life of someone who allows offence and bitterness to grow in him.

Boots of anger! An offended person is full of rage and anger.

A shield of hatred! You cannot stay a few minutes in the presence of an offended person without noticing the hatred they have.

A sword of bitterness! Mercy*! Bitterness is the convoluted version of unforgiveness.

A helmet of pride! A head filled with pride is indeed a head about to be cut off!

A hammer of revenge! Indeed, offended people are full of malice and ill-will, seeking an opportunity to revenge on the person they think has done them wrong.

Watch out for offended people. They are filled with devils and they are under full inspiration from hell!

---

* The author's colloquial expression

CHAPTER 18

Offences: How to Overcome Them

These things have I spoken unto you, that ye should not be offended.

John 16:1

1. **Expect to be offended in the ministry.**

   Woe unto the world because of offences! For it must needs be that offences come; but woe to that man by whom the offence cometh!

   Matthew 18:7

   Expect to be offended in the church. Jesus was emphatic that we would be hurt and offended. It would be nice if you were never offended about anything. It would be nice if your church were so perfect that nothing ever offended anyone. It would be nice if you had such good leadership skills that you were able to prevent any offence at all. Indeed, that would be simply amazing. But as long as you are on this earth, you will be offended at one point or the other.

   I struggle to accept in myself that I am offended. It is natural for me to declare that I have no offence in me. Indeed, I pride myself in saying that many things don't bother me deeply. I'm sure you are like that too. But even as I write, I can think of two people whose actions and words have disturbed me for months on end. Their behaviour keeps coming up to me as a bad smell from rotten meat. Try as I may, I can't seem to be happy with them and I wish they hadn't done the things they had done. My spirit is not at ease when I think deeply about their lives. I believe that I am offended in my soul at their treachery towards me.

   I can see why a person would keep on denying that he is offended. I don't like to admit that I'm offended with these people. It's like admitting to a very low mistake. However, if Jesus said we would be offended, it is my duty to accept that I am offended when it happens to me.

2. **Expect to be offended by a close person.**

   He saith unto him the third time, Simon, son of Jonas, lovest thou me? Peter was grieved because he said unto him the third time, Lovest thou me? And he said unto

him, Lord, thou knowest all things; thou knowest that I love thee. Jesus saith unto him, feed my sheep.

John 21:17

Only someone precious to me can offend me. It is only someone that you hold dear that will offend you. Most of the things you claim do not hurt you are things that are not close enough to hurt you deeply. Satan knows someone who is close to you and can really get to you. Expect to be offended by someone close and someone precious and someone dear to you.

Peter was close to Jesus. His denial of Jesus was truly painful. Jesus asked him the same question three times. Do you love me? Jesus was truly stunned by Peter claiming he had never seen nor interacted with Jesus before. Peter acted in this offensive way three times and Jesus also asked him three times if he loved Him.

You can be stunned by those closest to you! There are times I have been shocked at the actions and words of those I trusted with my life. Indeed I can only say that people who offend are capable of causing astonishment and bewilderment that will last a long time. A blow from a loved one can knock you out and lead to a loss of consciousness or strength. That's what it means to receive a stunning blow from your dear ones.

Expect stunning blows in the ministry! Look closely at your closest friends and aides. Look at them closely because they will be the source of your greatest help and also the source of your greatest pain.

Indeed, many ministers of the gospel have spouses who are their greatest helpers and also the source of their greatest pain. This paradox is part of ministry and part of life.

3. Confess and accept that you are offended.

If we say that we have no sin, we deceive ourselves, and the truth is not in us. If we confess our sins, he is faithful and just to forgive us our sins, and to cleanse

us from all unrighteousness. **If we say that we have not sinned, we make him a liar, and his word is not in us.**

1 John 1:8-10

Satan's greatest trick is to make you say you have no problem. It's to make you say I have no sin. It is to make you say, "I am not offended." Why is that? Satan's aim is to keep you self-deceived and lost in darkness. To do this, he has to keep you saying to yourself, "I am not offended. I am not hurt. I have forgiven them. I don't have a problem!"

If we say we have no offence, we deceive ourselves. Deceiving yourself is a bad thing. To deceive yourself is to continue in satan's grip. If you say you have no sin, you make God a liar. You actually insult God when you continually claim innocence.

Most people who are offended do not accept that they are actually offended, because there is a stigma attached to offence. Many deny that they are offended. It's amazing how easy it is for outsiders to see through your smoke screen and quickly conclude that you are offended.

One day some people rose up against me and said many evil things about me. Their declarations against me were noised abroad and many heard of their complaints and issues. A psychiatrist who was not a member of our church and who lived in America read their stories and their slander against me. The psychiatrist's comment about them was short and precise. He said, "I see a lot of hurt! I see hurting people! I see men with a lot of offence!"

However, these hurting people denied ever being hurt. Indeed, they claimed they were fighting injustice in the church. Other senior pastors urged these young men to overcome their hurts and offences. But they could not see any hurts and offences in themselves.

You see, outsiders can see through your hurts and offences. It's easy to see an offended person.

Offences: How to Overcome Them

4. Recognize that you are in danger when offended.

To whom ye forgive any thing, I forgive also: for if I forgave any thing, to whom I forgave it, for your sakes forgave I it in the person of Christ; Lest Satan should get an advantage of us: for we are not ignorant of his devices.

2 Corinthians 2:10-11

People who are offended are in great danger. In danger of what? They are in danger of satan taking advantage of their offence.

How does satan take advantage of an offence?

Satan is looking at your heart. He is looking closely to see if the wounds he has helped to inflict on you have become gaping access points for him. Once he sees infections and suppurations in the wound he will summon other demons to take advantage of the gap and enter in.

Satan waits to take advantage of your wounds. Satan's ability to take advantage of your wounds is what the scripture warns against. Once you are wounded, you are in danger of several more demonic attacks. Your heavily guarded life that has hitherto been well guarded can now be penetrated by devils. That is why every offending experience must put you on the alert. Like Apostle Paul, you must be keenly aware of the potential that hurt has to offend you.

But if any have caused grief, he hath not grieved me, but in part: that I may not overcharge you all. Sufficient to such a man is this punishment, which was inflicted of many. So that contrariwise ye ought rather to forgive him, and comfort him, lest perhaps such a one should be swallowed up with overmuch sorrow. Wherefore I beseech you that ye would confirm your love toward him. For to this end also did I write, that I might know the proof of you, whether ye be obedient in all things. To whom ye forgive any thing, I forgive also: for if I forgave any thing, to whom I forgave it, for your sakes forgave I it in the person of Christ; Lest Satan should get an advantage of us: for we are not ignorant of his devices.

2 Corinthians 2:5-11

5. Decide never to revenge.

Dearly beloved, avenge not yourselves, but rather give place unto wrath: for it is written, Vengeance is mine; I will repay, saith the Lord. Therefore if thine enemy hunger, feed him; if he thirst, give him drink: for in so doing thou shalt heap coals of fire on his head. Be not overcome of evil, but overcome evil with good.

Romans 12:19-21

Become spiritual and see things in God's way. Decide never to revenge on anyone that has wronged you. You will be wronged and hurt in such a way that you could fire back; but decide never to revenge or avenge yourself. God is the avenger! He is better at exacting revenge than you will ever be. He has asked that you leave those aspects to Him.

Indeed, getting involved and trying to exact some revenge on your enemies causes you to get in God's way. That is why He says, "Give place into wrath."

In other words, allow room for God to get involved and pay back for you. You will never able to lower your enemies the way God will lower them.

That no man go beyond and defraud his brother in any matter: because that the Lord is the avenger of all such, as we also have forewarned you and testified.

1 Thessalonians 4:6

The Lord is the avenger. He can avenge! He will avenge! He does avenge! He is the avenger! Leave it to Him and He will do it!

In the times that I have been fooled and mistreated by people I have learnt that it takes faith to believe that God will avenge. It is a stage in your walk with God to have to trust Him for revenge. Trusting God to avenge you starts by deciding to never get involved in punishing or hurting the offending person. Leave them entirely to God and to His timing for revenge.

6. Forgive quickly.

And when the sabbath was past, Mary Magdalene, and Mary the mother of James, and Salome, had bought sweet spices, that they might come and anoint him. And very early in the morning the first day of the week, they came unto the sepulchre at the rising of the sun. And they said among themselves, who shall roll us away the stone from the door of the sepulchre? And when they looked, they saw that the stone was rolled away: for it was very great. And entering into the sepulchre, they saw a young man sitting on the right side, clothed in a long white garment; and they were affrighted. And he saith unto them, Be not affrighted: Ye seek Jesus of Nazareth, which was crucified: he is risen; he is not here: behold the place where they laid him. But go your way, tell his disciples and Peter that he goeth before you into Galilee: there shall ye see him, as he said unto you.

Mark 16:1-7

Jesus gives the great example of forgiving quickly and restoring quickly. Even though Peter had denied ever knowing Jesus, He called back for him in just three days. Peter was Jesus' rock and appointed leader of the church. Peter was Jesus' contact man on earth. Peter threw Jesus to the dogs when he claimed he didn't know him on three different occasions. Yet Jesus still wanted to see Peter. The angel delivered a special message to the ladies - "Tell the disciples to meet me"; and Peter's name was mentioned specifically. Jesus seemed to have already forgiven Peter for his mess.

May God help us to also forgive quickly when the time comes to forgive!

Jesus also restored Peter to his position as the head of the church. Within six weeks Peter was back in charge and preaching powerfully on the Day of Pentecost. All the mistakes of the past were forgiven. Jesus seemed to restore Peter quite effortlessly and swiftly.

How Can I Forgive?

So then how can I forgive and what does it mean to forgive?

To forgive is to release all hurts bitterness and wickedness from your heart in such a way that satan stares in shock at a closed door to your heart. To forgive is to deny access to a horde of demons that are waiting. These are seven things to do that will constitute forgiveness.

a. Dismiss the issues that are thorny and painful.
b. Give up all claims against the person who has offended you.
c. Cancel any indebtedness towards the offending person.
d. Make no more mention of the matter that has offended you.
e. Stop feeling resentment against a particular person.
f. Stop feeling angry towards the one who offended you.
g. Cancel all punishments that you have planned for the person.

And be ye kind one to another, tenderhearted, forgiving one another, even as God for Christ's sake hath forgiven you.

Ephesians 4:32

7. Walk in love and pray for your offenders.

But I say unto you, Love your enemies, bless them that curse you, do good to them that hate you, and pray for them which despitefully use you, and persecute you; That ye may be the children of your Father which is in heaven: for he maketh his sun to rise on the evil and on the good, and sendeth rain on the just and on the unjust.

> Matthew 5:44-45

Praying for your offenders proves that you are walking in love. Instead of telling you to love your offenders, I am saying you should pray for those who offend you. Praying for someone who is attacking you is a revelation of your love for them.

You cannot pray genuinely for someone you hate. It's not easy to pray for someone you regard as an enemy. It is possible to say with your mouth that you love your brother. That's easy. However, no one can truly tell that you love them! Love is an invisible force that we all claim to possess. Christians fight and hurt each other all the time. Meanwhile each side claims to be walking in the love of God.

Therefore when they were gathered together, Pilate said unto them, whom will ye that I release unto you? Barabbas, or Jesus which is called Christ? For he knew that for envy they had delivered him.

> Matthew 27:17-18

I have come to be wary when I am told that a person is a Christian. I am always concerned that I will encounter an envious Christian. An envious Christian is like a dangerous human devil. Indeed envious Christians can be even more antagonistic and hateful. There is actually a lot of jealousy and envy in the church and that accounts for many of the conflicts that Christians encounter. Jesus Christ was crucified and tortured because of envy in religious people. You must indeed fear envious, religious people. If you are more prosperous than those around you, you must assume that they are envious of you until proved otherwise.

Remember that when Jesus was on the cross and being offended greatly by the wickedness, rejection and ungratefulness of the Jewish nation, He actually prayed for them.

Then said Jesus, Father, forgive them; for they know not what they do. And they parted his raiment, and cast lots.

Luke 23:34

It's time to check and see whether you can offer a genuine prayer for certain people. Remember that you are equally in dire need of forgiveness from God.

For if you forgive men their trespasses your heavenly father will also forgive you:

Matthew 6:14

Seventy per cent of love is made up of forgiveness. If you love someone it means you forgive the person. It's time to accept that you must walk in love and forgive anyone who has offended you. Check your forgiveness checklist again if you claim you are walking in love.

a. Have you dismissed the issues that are thorny and painful to you?

b. Have you given up all claims against the person who has offended you?

c. Have you cancelled any indebtedness of the one who hurt you?

d. Do you still make mention of the matter that has offended you?

e. Have you stopped feeling resentment against your offender?
f. Have you stopped feeling angry towards the one who hurt you?

g. Have you cancelled all punishments and revenge you have planned for those who hurt you?

If you follow these steps you will be free from hurts!

CHAPTER 19

How to Protect Yourself from Being Offended

These things have I spoken unto you, that ye should not be offended.

John 16:1

Offended people are badly hurt. Offended people are hurting and smarting from things that have happened in their lives. Offence is unavoidable in your journey with God. There are several things that Jesus mentioned in His discourse to the disciples that will protect you from becoming offended one day.

Offence is headed directly for you. Offence will destroy the greatest apostle and spoil the most faithful pastor. Offence will derail the destinies of many God-lovers. Therefore if there is anything to protect you from this terrible and unavoidable evil, you must grasp it.

Jesus said clearly in John 16:1 that He had told His disciples certain things that would protect them from falling from offence. There are things that you can hear that will help to protect you from offence in the day you become a candidate for offence. Arming your mind with certain realities about the future and believing that certain things will happen, will stabilize you when Satan attacks you in order to offend you.

Forasmuch then as Christ hath suffered for us in the flesh, arm yourselves likewise with the same mind: for he that hath suffered in the flesh hath ceased from sin;

1 Peter 4:1

No one is offended by good things! No one is offended or affected negatively when good things are happening. It is when the negative experiences of ministry occur that minds begin to change. People can do a U-turn when they have negative experiences. Jesus wanted His disciples to expect and anticipate the horror of hatred, persecution and rampant demonic activity. It would change the atmosphere and cause a bad feeling in the church. People would leave, abandon ship and turn into traitors because of these experiences. Bad experiences always offend people and can easily turn them into traitors and disloyal men.

And then shall many be offended, and shall betray one another, and shall hate one another.

Matthew 24:10

The first verse of John chapter sixteen gives us the protection from offence. We must also look deeply into the fourteenth and fifteenth chapters of John for the secrets that will protect us from offence. Indeed in these chapters we see things that Jesus predicted and expected us to have in our minds.

Jesus armed the minds of His disciples to protect them from becoming offended. You must believe the following truths that Jesus gives and they will help you and save you from offence.

1. **EXPECT AN EXPERIENCE OF PRESSURE AND TROUBLE AND DONT LET IT OFFEND OR AFFECT YOU.**

   These things I have spoken unto you, that in me ye might have peace. In the world ye shall have tribulation: but be of good cheer; I have overcome the world.

   John 16:33

   The word tribulation means trouble, pressures, difficulties, burdens and anguish. It is important to expect these things and survive them when they happen. It's amazing how many people change into monsters when they experience pressure, trouble or difficulty.

   Jesus predicted tribulation for His disciples and warned them not to change or turn around. Do not turn into a traitor because of difficulties or challenges. Some people cannot take the pressure or challenge of change. Some people cannot take the pressure or challenge of being transferred to another location. Some people cannot take the pressure or financial challenges of life and ministry. There are pressures, challenges, and difficulties in this world.

2. **EXPECT AN EXPERIENCE OF PURGING AND DON'T LET IT OFFEND OR AFFECT YOU.**

   I am the true vine, and my Father is the husbandman. Every branch in me that beareth not fruit he taketh away:

and every branch that beareth fruit, he purgeth it, that it may bring forth more fruit.

John 15:1-2

When there is a season of purging many people will be cleared out of the system. God believes in purging! God purges ministries ever so often. Expect a purge in your ministry very soon. Purges are good because they allow for new and fresh growth. A divine purge is necessary and many times the ministry cannot continue with certain people present.

Usually people are purged out when they are offended. They think they are offended and walk away in righteous indignation. But actually they are being purged out of the church by the Lord. God does not intend to carry on with them. The train moves on but without them. Pray that you will not be purged out by offences. Beware of offences! It may be a season in which you will be plucked out and removed from a certain family in order to purify it and cleanse it of your presence! Amazing! May you not be the unwanted element that needs to be flushed out of a church to make it grow even bigger and better.

I have seen many purges in my ministry. The people purged out of the church were often significant people who were rotten within and needed to be removed from the team. These people needed to excuse themslves so we could move on. Most of the time they were offended and walked away in indignation hurling accusations and insinuations at us.

3. AN EXPERIENCE OF HATRED FROM THE WORLD WILL OFFEND YOU AND AFFECT YOU.

. If the world hate you, ye know that it hated me before it hated you.

John 15:18

Hatred is a terrible feeling to experience. Hatred is the most extreme negative feeling you can have from a fellow human being. Do not be surprised that you have these extreme reactions from people just because of the ministry. I know quite a few people who hate me because of my ministry. The mention of my name stirs up extreme anger and hatred towards me and my church. However their hatred does not put me off or make me stop what I am doing in the ministry. I wish they didn't hate me but I have had to get used to the idea of people hating me. It's a very uncomfortable feeling indeed to be hated by people. Don't let the rise of hatred destroy your ministry or put you off. Fighting hateful people is part of the things you must expect to do as part of your ministry.

4. HATRED WITHOUT A CAUSE WILL OFFEND YOU AND AFFECT YOU.

If I had not done among them the works which none other man did, they had not had sin: but now have they both seen and hated both me and my Father. But this cometh to pass, that the word might be fulfilled that is written in their law, They hated me without a cause.

John 15:24-25

Hatred without a cause is an even more puzzling experience. "Why does this person hate me?" That's a question I have asked myself many times. I have encountered outsiders who have never met me or ever spoken to me before. Yet they are filled with a passionate hatred for me and my ministry. This is what Jesus experienced and ended up being crucified by people who didn't even know what He believed or taught. Get ready for all these experiences and make sure you are not bumped off by wicked and unreasonable men.

5. AN EXPERIENCE OF PERSECUTION WILL OFFEND YOU AND AFFECT YOU.

Remember the word that I said unto you, The servant is not greater than his lord. If they have persecuted me, they will also persecute you; if they have kept my saying, they will keep yours also.

John 15:20

There will be those who take up a fight with you as their main work - people employed by satan to do nothing but oppose and fight you. Do not be turned away from the ministry by anyone's persecution of you. Do not be surprised that you are harassed by your family, friends or loved ones. These are often common reasons for being offended. Expect to have family problems and various challenges with people that can redirect your whole life and ministry.

6. AN EXPERIENCE OF REJECTION.

They shall put you out of the synagogues: yea, the time cometh, that whosoever killeth you will think that he doeth God service.

John 16:2

Rejection is an experience of being on the outside and looking on at a group that seem to be specially favoured. It's a terrible experience of not really being wanted but just being tolerated by people. Rejection is one of the commonest causes of offence. You must steel your heart to experience rejection over and over again.

I smile to myself as I write this because I can think of many different groups to which I belong but don't really want me. I feel like an outsider and an unwanted foreigner in many situations. It's a pity that we should ever have to suffer rejection. Do not let any feelings of being an outsider direct your ministry!

We are all outsiders and we are all unwanted in one way or another. Remember that Jesus was rejected much more than any other person. By an astonishing and an incredulous decision ever to be taken by human beings, Jesus was rejected by the Jewish society of Jerusalem and Barabbas was preferred. Jesus must have looked on in amazement over the crowd that rejected Him and chose Barabbas instead of Him.

7. INVASION OF DEMONIC ACTIVITY.

Hereafter I will not talk much with you: for the prince of this world cometh, and hath nothing in me.

John 14:30

Strong demonic attacks usually cause a fallout to occur. Expect an onslaught of demonic activities. When there is a strong work of demons in your church it will cause many things to happen and one of them is offence. As the demons multiply in the church, there is strife, confusion and every evil work. Where you notice strife, quarrels and confusion, you must accept that there are demons present, stirring things up.

Conclusion

Jesus Christ is the greatest Prophet that ever lived! He predicted that hurts and offences would come to everyone.

Hurts and offences have caused too much devastation in the church. It is my prayer that with these few words you will be delivered from the evil and the curse that comes through offence.

And further, by these, my son, be admonished: of making many books there is no end; and much study is a weariness of the flesh!

Books by Dag Heward-Mills

1. Loyalty and Disloyalty
2. Those Who Accuse You
3. Those Who are Proud
4. Those Who are Dangerous Sons
5. Those Who are Ignorant
6. Those Who Forget
7. Those Who Leave You
8. Those Who Pretend
9. One of You is a Devil
10. Church Planting
11. Church Growth ...*It Is Possible!*
12. The Mega Church, 2nd Ed
13. Amplify Your Ministry with Miracles and Manifestations of The Holy Spirit
14. Laikos - *Lay People and the Ministry*
15. Steps to The Anointing
16. Sweet Influences of The Anointing
17. Catch the Anointing
18. The Anointed and His Anointing
19. Transform Your Pastoral Ministry
20. The Art of Shepherding
21. What it Means to Become a Shepherd
22. The Art of Following
23. The Art of Hearing, 2nd Ed
24. The Art of Leadership, 3rd Ed
25. A Good General...*The Science of Leadership*
26. Anagkazo - *Compelling Power*
27. Others....
28. Tell Them - *120 Reasons Why You Must be a Soul Winner*
29. How You Can Preach Salvation
30. What it Means to be as Wise as a Serpent
31. Many Are Called
32. How You Can Make Full Proof of Your Ministry
33. The Top 10 Mistakes Pastors Make
34. How to Neutralize Curses
35. Victory Secrets
36. Losing, Suffering, Sacrificing & Dying
37. It is a Great thing to Serve the Lord
38. Ministerial Ethics, 2nd Ed
39. Why Non-Tithing Christians Become Poor and How Tithing Christians Can Become Rich
40. He that Hath, To Him Shall be Given: and He That Hath Not, From Him Shall Be Taken Even That Which He Hath
41. Model Marriage
42. The Beauty, The Beast and The Pastor
43. Rules of Church Work
44. Rules of Full-time Ministry
45. Church Administration
46. How to Pray
47. Name it! Claim it!! Take it!!!
48. 100% Answered Prayer
49. Forgiveness made Easy, 3rd Ed
50. Demons and How to Deal With Them

51. Spiritual Dangers
52. Blood Power - *The Blood of Jesus*
53. How to Be Born Again and Avoid Hell
54. Read your Bible, Pray Everyday ...*if You Want to Grow*
55. How You Can Become a Strong Christian
56. How You Can Have an Effective Quiet Time with God Everyday
57. Backsliding - *Develop Your Staying Power*
58. Daughter You Can Make It
59. The Tree and Your Ministry
60. Know Your Invisible Enemies ...*and defeat them*
61. Make Yourselves Saviours of Men
62. Everything by Prayer, Nothing Without Prayer
63. The Determinants
64. Attempt Great Things for God
65. Can't You Do Just a Little Bit More?
66. Seven Great Principles, 2nd Ed
67. Steps to God's Presence
68. The Double Mega Missionary Church
69. Labour to be Blessed ...*Labour Not to be Rich*
70. Those Who Honour You
71. The Anointing and The Presence
72. Faith Secrets
73. Flow in the Anointing
74. Flow Prayer Book
75. The Preparation of the Gospel
76. How Can I Say Thanks
77. Bema - *Judgment and Justice*
78. Fruitfulness
79. 1000 Micro Churches
80. Why Few are Chosen
81. Lord I Know You Need Somebody
82. The Privilege
83. The Gift of Governments
84. Wisdom is the Principal Thing For Your Ministry
85. Predestination
86. Ministerial Barrenness
87. If You Love the Lord
88. Ready @ 20
89. Enlargement Secrets
90. Am I Good for Nothing?
91. Be Thou Faithful Unto Death
92. Going Deeper and Doing More
93. Tasters and Partakers
94. Weeping and Gnashing
95. Not a Novice
96. Stir it Up
97. Seeing and Hearing
98. The Church Must Send or it Will End
99. The Word of My Patience
100. Those Who Are Offended

Resources by the author can be found at:
daghewardmillsbooks.org ; daghewardmillsvideos.org ; daghewardmillsaudio.org

Download and listen to the **Dag Heward-Mills daily podcast** on your preferred podcast source.